To Mary –

Wings to Rise: Blacks, Leadership, and the Assemblies of God

Stay Faithful
to the
Lord!

† Darnell Williams

"The heartbeat of Dr. Darnell Williams is expressed clearly, with supporting research documentation, challenging the Assemblies of God as a whole to play a role in ending the conspicuous absence of black leadership in key positions throughout the Fellowship. Dr. Williams' research supports the fact that the AG, along with other religious institutions, played a major role in the history of a segregated American Church that contributed to the legacy of racial hatred still very present in America today. He challenges the Church to wake up and realize that it is not too late to repent and do what is right before God and humanity. It is my prayer that the Assemblies of God, a Fellowship I love, will once again believe, 'That the color line has been washed away in the blood of Jesus,' by embracing the advice of Dr. Williams."

—Rev. Dr. Zollie L. Smith
Retired Pastor and Executive Officer
Executive Director, Assemblies of God U.S. Missions (2007-2017)
Inaugural President, National Black Fellowship (1998-2007)
AG General Council Executive Presbyter, Ethnic Fellowships
Asst. Superintendent and Executive Secretary, New Jersey AG District

Dr. Darnell Williams is an apostolic architecture. In his new book, he, like the Apostle Paul, masterfully builds bridges upon the foundation of Christ, biblical history, and practical principles of intention mentoring and empowering. This book is a manual for strengthening any person, church, denominational office or organization through equitable diversity inclusion.

—Bishop Walter Harvey
President, National Black Fellowship of the Assemblies of God

"Dr. Williams's doctoral project is indeed worthy of broad circulation, and I am very pleased to see this is now a possibility with its transformation into a readable book, *Wings to Rise*. The depth of his study and insight is here presented in his usual stellar form of communication. It allows for the reader to learn, think, and be transformed. Moving blacks and other groups into representation around the leadership table is our next *sine qua non*. I do not believe we can legitimately move forward without it. *Wings to Rise* is both motivational and practical in providing pathway ideas for getting it done."

—Rev. Dr. Carolyn Tennant
Professor Emerita, North Central University, Minneapolis, MN and
Adjunct Professor, Assemblies of God Theological Seminary

"The relationship of the Church of God in Christ and the Assemblies of God reaches beyond 100 years ago. The story of the historic meeting in 1913 in Hot Springs, Arkansas is known to any leader of either denomination. However, in the years following 1913, the story of the Black churches and ministers within the Assemblies of God Church is not widely known. I look forward to learning more about the subject through this tremendous book by Bishop Darnell K. Williams. It is my pleasure to give this endorsement."

—Rev. Charles E. Blake, Sr.
Presiding Bishop,
Church of God in Christ International

"Bishop Williams has cast a vision. Imagine '...a shift from organic growth of minority leaders to intentional cultivation.' The gates of hell would be shattered by such a shift. One hundred years of Assemblies of God organic "growth" has yielded only a handful of elected district/network and national level black officers. Organic alone is not working. It's time for a shift."

—Rev. Christopher N. Beard
Lead Pastor, Peoples Church Cincinnati AG
General Presbyter, Ohio Ministry Network AG

"The 'moment' resulting from the George Floyd tragedy has reopened a long-standing wound in our nation. Anger, shrill rhetoric, and upheaval may be a predictable part of this season. However, a hope-filled way forward for the Assemblies of God has been provided by Dr. Darnell Williams. Biblical foundations, cultural acuity, and practical strategies are joined to yield pathways for healing, reconciliation, and enduring empowerment for all God's people. *Wings to Rise* is a gift to the Assemblies of God that can strengthen our efforts to represent Christ's Kingdom rule in powerful and visible ways."

—Rev. Dr. Byron D. Klaus
President, Assemblies of God Theological Seminary (1999-2015)

"Transforming a barrier into an opportunity is a major task. Yet transformation can happen as people are willing to hear truth, clarify the reality of the current, develop solution steps, and embrace the sacrifice needed for successful change. Information empowers; the *right* information can create exponential empower, but *only truth* brings freedom. In *Wings to Rise*, Dr. Williams boldly shares the truths of a well-defined path toward an improved future of racial inclusion and diversity in any leadership team. He writes with focused purpose and challenges status quo thinking. I believe this book has the potential to mold an inclusive generation of leaders who will bring variety in wisdom, experience and vision."

—Rev. Scott Holmes
Network Superintendent, Louisiana Assemblies of God

"In this book, Dr. Darnell Williams has not only named the issues facing the Assemblies of God regarding race, but he has outlined specific steps that every pastor and district leader should embrace and implement immediately. If the strategies in this book are implemented throughout the AG USA, it will accelerate the healing of the wounds of racism that have hindered the full move of God within the fellowship."

—Rev. Dr. Shannon Polk, Esq.

"Flying is counterintuitive and exposes our fear of heights. However, for the individual who conquers their fear, freedom is the reward. As leaders, many of us remember the mentor who taught us how to fly—the man or woman who stood behind us and pushed us toward greatness and walked us through our fears. Dr. Williams in his book, *Wings to Rise*, calls his readers to become intentional pushers—to elevate the forgotten, resource the marginalized, and empower the powerless. He reminds us that people are God's most precious resource, and if we keep that in mind, there is continued hope for the relevancy of American Pentecostalism. *Wings to Rise* has renewed my passion as a leader to invest myself into young leaders of color. Watching them fly for the first time is my reward for being a pusher."

—Rev. Dr. Samuel M. Huddleston
Assistant District Superintendent,
Northern California and Nevada District
Author, *Five Years to Life*

"What a timely word for our Fellowship during this season of racial unrest and cultural divisions. Darnell shows us the need for a greater diverse environment within our churches. He says the Holy Spirit is leading us to cultivate leaders within our communities and churches by 'intentionally elevating the forgotten and those living in the shadows.' The only hope for a divided nation is a diverse and racially united church.

—Rev. Malcolm Burleigh
Executive Director, Assemblies of God U.S. Missions

"Incorporating black people into senior leadership of classical Pentecostal denominational hierarchies has been the Achilles' heel for churches in the western hemisphere. The Assemblies of God, the largest Pentecostal denomination in the world, has been a global mission force with a giant footprint in Africa. In spite of the intercultural flowering of the AG around the world, however, it has remained predominantly white at the executive leadership level. In this timely book, Darnell Williams, an ordained minister and executive presbyter in the Assemblies of God, provides us with a compelling analysis of how inclusive leadership from a biblical and theological perspective should be nurtured. Williams points a way forward toward a new leadership future for the AG—and other classical Pentecostal denominations in the West—in which blacks are included at every level."

—Rev. Dr. Clifton R. Clarke
Research Fellow,
Queen's Foundation for Ecumenical Theological Education
Ordained Bishop, Church of God Cleveland

"Rev. Dr. Darnell K. Williams, Sr., a leading voice in the international community at large and in the African American community, does a masterful job in his foundational work, *Wings to Rise: Blacks, Leadership, and the Assemblies of God.* He presents the biblical and historical foundation for a multicultural church in a diverse world. Dr. Williams demonstrates the need for ethnic diversity at every level of leadership, providing a viable voice for every nation under heaven. His voice calling for ethnic leadership representation is loud and clear, but gracious and respectful, bringing balance and reason to a world that all too often has forgotten how to communicate responsibly. Perhaps his greatest contribution is answering the question of how we practically address the racial disparity not only in the world but in the church at large. Dr. Williams' book is a must-read, not only for the AG but for all Christians everywhere serious about the inclusion of godly leaders at every level from every people group. It is a joy to wholeheartedly endorse his epic research as a prophetic voice to the nations."

—Rev. W. A. Mills, Jr.
Director, IPHC Men's Ministries

"As a leadership strategist, I consult both ministry and marketplace leaders, from Wall Street to Silicon Valley, and they too are wrestling with the very same question examined in this prophetic work—how do we create more space for diversity in leadership? While Dr. Williams has written a timely primer around blacks and leadership in the Assemblies of God, he may have inadvertently authored a must-read book for Christian leaders across denominations. He proves biblically why both space and pathways to leadership roles must be created for blacks for the sake of the gospel, the witness of the Church, and the winning of younger generations. Fortunately, Dr. Williams not only proves *why* but show us *how* to do so. Read this book, follow its principles, and generations from now your work will be remembered."

—Dr. Don Brawley III
President, Influencers Global

Wings to Rise is a far-reaching book for these current times as we navigate through biblical values, racial tensions, ecclesiastical conversations, and this God moment. This publication is theologically sound, academically insightful in its research, and practically solid in its applicable steps that will guide an organization, enterprise, or ministry into a new space and place in an increasingly diverse community and world as we reflect on the past, correct former mistakes, and project vision, actions, and practices for a new preferred future.

—Bishop Lafayette Scales
Lead Pastor, Rhema Christian Center, Columbus, Ohio
Bishop, The Network of Local Churches

Wings to Rise: Blacks, Leadership, and the Assemblies of God

Darnell K. Williams, Sr.

Foreword by
Doug Clay

WINGS TO RISE: BLACKS, LEADERSHIP, AND THE ASSEMBLIES OF
GOD

ISBN 13: 978-0-578-80204-6

Cataloguing-in-Publication Data

Wings to Rise: Blacks, Leadership, and the Assemblies of God; foreword by Doug
Clay.

xxxiii + 133 p. ; 23 cm. Includes bibliographical references.
ISBN 13: 978-0-578-80204-6
I. Williams, Darnell K. Sr. II. Clay, Doug.
III. Wings to Rise: Blacks, Leadership, and the Assemblies of God.

CALL NUMBER 2020

Manufactured in the U.S.A.   2020

Dedication

To My Mother – Gwendolyn Delores Williams-Russell

Table of Contents

Foreword

The history of the Assemblies of God is a continuous story of ordinary people through whom God accomplishes extraordinary things. *Wings to Rise* is another great example of this. The book you are about to read represents a young man who grew up in a single-parent home and pushed past all the challenges of his childhood to become a leader of influence in the kingdom of God.

Dr. Darnell Williams has brilliantly taken the academic work of his doctoral research and blended it with his own personal experience to provide an outstanding, biblically based resource to assist churches in becoming more inclusive in leadership.

At the time of this book's publishing (2020), 44 percent of the U.S. Assemblies of God adherents are ethnic minorities, making our Fellowship more diverse than the U.S. population as a whole. If trends continue, it is possible that the Assemblies of God will be a Movement with no ethnic majority in a few years. I believe *Wings to Rise* will help our Fellowship achieve this goal.

As you read *Wings to Rise*, may a spirit of intentionality grow in you as you cultivate diverse leadership in the ministry you lead.

—Doug Clay, General Superintendent
of the Assemblies of God USA

Preface

I am an ordained minister with the Assemblies of God (AG) and serve as lead pastor of New Life Church International (NLCI), a diverse church racially: 60 percent African American, 20 percent white, and 20 percent black immigrant (West Africa and West Indies). NLCI demonstrates its diverse nature socio-economically as well, attracting educated professionals, middle-class workers, and those facing economic challenges.

Since 2014, I have also served as secretary-treasurer of the International Ministry Network (IMN), formerly known as the German District of the Assemblies of God (GDAG). By virtue of my office, I serve on the General Presbytery. Founded in 1922 and structured as a language district, the GDAG held a presence across the United States as it served its mission of reaching German immigrants. In recent years, however, the GDAG has undergone a radical transformation.

As the nation's landscape shifted throughout the twentieth century and later generations emerged, the district lost momentum. Geographic districts began absorbing most GDAG churches. When the district elected Dan Miller as their superintendent in 2007, Miller initially thought his assignment would be to close the fading district of eleven churches and twenty-five credential holders. As vision for church planting began to rise within his heart, however, he began attracting young leaders who had a heart for urban ministry, many of whom are African American. Rebranded as the International Ministry Network (IMN), the district now has over one hundred credential holders and thirty-two churches across the United States.[1] The vast majority of these churches are multicultural along with congregations of international immigrants as well. The network currently holds the designation of a language district while enjoying the same privileges as a geographic district. This gives the network a national presence, allowing it to have churches across geographic lines and in all fifty states.

In addition to these roles, I have also served as an executive of the National Black Fellowship (NBF) since 2013, first as executive treasurer (2013 to 2018) and then as vice president (2018 to present). The NBF remains one of twenty-two ethnic fellowships recognized by the Assemblies of God. The vision of NBF is to "recruit, develop, and empower ministers and churches to fulfill God's mission in urban America."[2] The NBF has the largest number of churches of any ethnic fellowship, with 432 total congregations.[3] In addition, at the fifty-eighth General Council of the Assemblies of God in August 2019, I was elected as an executive presbyter, serving on the highest governance body in the organization.

The United States Assemblies of God has been celebrated as one of the most diverse Christian organizations in America, nearly mirroring the nation's ethnic population demographically. This diversity has emerged from the growth and development of multi-ethnic congregations, as well as the expansion of black, Spanish-speaking, Asian, and various immigrant congregations. Despite the healthy diversity within the constituency of the Assemblies of God, however, an overall lack of diversity within AG district leadership prevails. Ordained credential holders are elected into positions of leadership at the AG district level. However, while the sixty-seven districts of the Fellowship may have African Americans serving at various levels of leadership, only two black individuals serve as duly elected district executives.

In response to the lack of diversity at this level, I sought in my doctoral research at the Assemblies of God Theological Seminary to cultivate pathways to recognize, appoint, promote, and ultimately elect African Americans into such positions of leadership. I began assessing the issue by conducting a set of interviews with innovative leaders. Further, I examined biblical principles foundational to placing minority leaders into positions of influence and reviewed contemporary literature to gain insights into successfully cultivating leaders of color, various ethnic backgrounds, and both genders. Following my research, I developed two appreciative inquiry (AI) workshops with the Great Lakes Regional Superintendents Cohort of the Assemblies of God in order to solicit input and grasp momentum for this endeavor.

This book provides the research and practical application conducted for my doctoral studies as a reproducible resource for ministry in order to cultivate opportunities for black leaders in the Assemblies of God. The Almighty designed birds to fly; it is in their nature and connected to their purpose. Without wings, they are doomed to an existence of frustration, being connected to the skies but never quite able to fly. Likewise, blacks can offer powerful partnership and perspectives as leaders. Our history, narrative, story and influence can assist the organization in achieving that which it has struggled to accomplish with our absence. My mother would often say, "I don't need you to carry me through; just open the doors, and I'll gladly walk through them." So, to blacks within the Assemblies: stand ready to serve as well as to lead; we just need the wings to rise.

---

[1] International Ministry Network, "Campus Locations," IMNF, accessed May 24, 2018, http://internationalministrynetwork.com/about-us/#our-locations.
[2] National Black Fellowship of the Assemblies of God, "Mission and Vision," NBAFG, accessed June 13, 2018, http://www.nbfag.org/about-us/mission--vision.
[3] General Council of the Assemblies of God, "2016 Race and Ethnicity Report," General Secretary's Office, June 6, 2017, accessed June 11, 2018, https://ag.org/About/Statistics.

Acknowledgments

I would like to begin by expressing my overwhelming gratitude to my Lord and Savior Jesus Christ, who found a hurting, lost, and purposeless sixteen-year-old boy and trusted him with a divine call. I feel like David of old, who God took from the pens to pastor His people (Ps 78:72). I never cease to marvel at what God has accomplished through a boy from the streets of Cleveland, Ohio, with every challenge against him. God helped me overcome!

I will forever remain indebted to my great cloud of witnesses: my great-grandmother, Mattie "Big Momma" Williams, who declared—even while I was still in the womb—that God had a plan for my life; my grandmother, Naomi "Madea" Williams, who took me to church as a boy; my dear aunt, Betty Louise Williams, who willingly made sacrifices to treat her nephews as her sons; and my dear mother, Gwendolyn Delores Williams-Russell, who began motherhood at sixteen years old and left this earth far too soon. Mom, your boys turned out okay! We took your training, and now both your sons have earned doctoral degrees. To my spiritual father and mentor, Bishop Burton Ross, "Dad Ross," thank you for being an example of a godly man who showed us more than you told us. Your quiet spirit, sincere love for Christ, and humility created a template for my life as a leader, minister, husband, and father. To my father, Larry Keith Darnell Davis: Pop, I now understand your pain and regret I couldn't do more as a son to help.

I also remain grateful beyond words for my "living epistles." The Lord blessed me when I found my soulmate and partner in life and ministry, Kim Charlene Williams. Your tireless words of encouragement and patience during this pursuit have made all the difference!

Though just two simple words, you understand the gravity of them—thank you! To my son, my namesake, Darnell Keith Adrian Williams, Jr., I live my life to demonstrate to you how to fulfill Micah 6:8. Son, never stop dreaming, and never stop pushing.

To my brother, Dr. Jason Matthew Williams, I am so proud of you. We did it! To my Aunt Sharon, thanks for always being there for me and giving me your words of affirmation. To my brothers-in-law, sisters-in-law, nieces, nephews, and extended family (Williams and Simmons), thank you for blessing my life. To my superintendent, Rev. Daniel J. Miller, Bishop Dan, thank you for helping me to dream again! Likewise, to the IMN family, thank you for granting me the opportunity to lead.

To my spiritual heroes, Dr. Samuel Huddleston, Rev. Malcolm Burleigh, and Rev. Zollie Smith, I am grateful for your servant leadership and for blessing my life. I also extend deep gratitude to my dear friends and fellow servants of the National Black Fellowship—Rev. Michael Nelson, Rev. Walter Harvey, Rev. Darrell Geddes, Rev. Gerard Ruff—for your unwavering support. To my covenant brother, Dr. Don Brawley, thank you for your faithful friendship. To Rev. Shawn Branham, who called me "Doctor" long before the reality came to pass, and to Rev. Andrew Ross and the Ross Family, thank you for loving me.

I also want to express my profound appreciation to the Assemblies of God Theological Seminary (AGTS) team, former D.Min. Director, Dr. Cheryl Taylor, who took time at a General Council to engage with me about this program; and former D.Min. Project Coordinator, Dr. Lois Olena, for patiently guiding me through the project phase. I also want to thank my instructors: Dr. Earl Creps, Dr. Don Detrick, Dr. Lori S. O'Dea, Dr. Doug Oss, Dr. Charlie Self, Dr. Jim Rion, Dr. Mike McCrary, and Dr. Bryon Klaus. I want to thank my biblical adviser, Dr. Jim Hernando, as well as express heartfelt appreciation to Dr. Carolyn Tennant, who served as my professor for two classes and who pastored me through the writing process as my project adviser. I also want to extend a special thanks to my editor, Erica Huinda—your skillfulness was invaluable! Thanks also goes to Dr. Jeff Fulks for his insightfulness and assistance in developing the Black Credential Holders Survey.

Finally, I offer deep gratitude to my New Life Church International family. The board of elders, administrative team, and lay leadership team who absorbed some of my duties created the necessary margin for enabling me to pursue this project to completion. To the NLCI congregation, thank you for trusting me to shepherd you.

Wings to Rise: Blacks, Leadership, and the Assemblies of God

Introduction

A Powerful Opportunity

As an Assemblies of God minister and pastor of a diverse congregation, a leader in a multicultural network that is 60 percent African American, an executive in the National Black Fellowship, which seeks to "recruit, develop and empower ministers and churches to fulfill God's mission in urban America," and an AG executive presbyter, I believe God has placed me in a unique position to help our movement cultivate a diverse leadership in order to reach a diverse America.

As the world's largest Protestant movement, the Assemblies of God has a powerful opportunity to leverage its influence to create pathways for African American leaders. The Assemblies of God has already proven itself as a global force in world missions. It has successfully sent forth missionaries to establish church networks, found Bible schools, and provide humanitarian outreach through healthcare, nutrition, and digging wells. With its missional focus and equipped ministers, it now has a remarkable opportunity to make significant impact in urban America.

This book has the potential to face the racial divide in the United States and to make a way forward to address the sin of institutional racism and individual prejudices that still plague the landscape of this nation. As people of color are empowered to positions of leadership in our Fellowship, they can lead the Church in overcoming racial division and pave the way for a radical spiritual renewal in the nation's urban centers, which remain plagued by poverty, violence, dysfunction, and hopelessness. This will require intentionality around the promotion of black individuals in roles of leadership at all levels of the Fellowship. This book is designed to cultivate such leadership, as it promotes the strides the AG has already made over the decades and further spurs the Fellowship to continue identifying, recruiting, promoting, appointing, electing, and making space for black leaders among its ranks.

The Pew Research Center noted in a 2015 study that the Assemblies of God has become the most diverse Protestant movement in the country.[1] The Fellowship largely mirrors the racial demographic makeup of the United States:

Demographic	United States[2] (stated as a percentage)	Assemblies of God[3] (stated as a percentage)
White	61.3	57.7
Black	13.3	10.1
Asian	5.7	4.8
Mix/Other	2.6	4.0
Hispanic	17.0	22.0

Despite the healthy diversity within the constituency of the Assemblies of God, a lack of diversity within leadership prevails. While the sixty-seven districts of the Fellowship may have African Americans serving at various levels of leadership, as of 2020, only two black individuals serve as duly elected district executives: Dr. Samuel Huddleston, who serves as assistant superintendent of the Northern California and Nevada District, and myself. The General Presbytery comprises district-elected executives, pastoral representatives from each district, and representatives of ethnic or language fellowships. As of 2014, 88 (32 percent) of the 274 general presbyters are ethnic or language GPs. Minority GP representation comes predominately from either ethnic fellowship representation or language districts rather than through elected district leaders.

Though the Fellowship remains racially diverse in terms of constituents, the leaders at the district levels do not reflect this diversity. As a result, black leaders are underrepresented in the current electoral process within the Assemblies of God, and an opportunity exists to cultivate diversity within leadership roles. This will require working with or around the governance model of the Fellowship, which is primarily based upon elected leadership. Because of this model, minorities face a daunting task to occupy leadership positions.

Action Steps

Introduction

To address these barriers and make the most of the opportunity before the Assemblies of God, I set out to cultivate and promote leadership opportunities for African Americans through a project associated with my Doctor of Ministry degree work at the Assemblies of God Theological Seminary. This work included a set of interviews with innovative leaders and two appreciative inquiry (AI) workshops with the Great Lakes Regional Superintendents Cohort of the Assemblies of God.[4]

This book contains the research and practical application of that endeavor and serves as a way forward for the AG in providing a strong biblical-theological foundation as well as practical steps for achieving this goal. The book presents realistic and actionable recommendations to create opportunities for African American leaders within the Assemblies of God. While conversations can speak to the sin of racism in the United States and in the history of Pentecostalism, I advocate here focusing on the path forward, using a proactive and pragmatic approach.

Interviews with Innovative Leaders

I commenced my interview process by meeting Assemblies of God General Superintendent Doug Clay in the spring of 2018. I had three objectives for that meeting: (1) to seek his support, input, and partnership in my endeavor; (2) to obtain a list of innovative leaders and pacesetters within the Fellowship active in the areas of inclusion, diversity, and multiethnic leadership; and (3) to discuss the merits of conducting workshops with the Great Lakes Regional Superintendents Cohort as the focus of my field research.

I conducted four of the interviews with innovative leaders at the Joint World Missions-U.S. Missions Retreat, which was held February 11-14, 2019. I conducted a fifth interview via telephone during that same month. During these interviews, I documented our conversations and searched for common themes among the innovative leaders.

Black Credential Holders Survey

I followed these interviews up with distribution of the Black Credential Holders Survey in August 2019 to ascertain the engagement of these leaders with leadership opportunities. I had created the survey for black credential holders to determine the perception of opportunities for African American leaders at the sectional, regional, district, and national levels. To obtain contact information, I contacted the statistics department of the AG General Secretary at the National Leadership and Resource Center for a list of black credential holders to facilitate the distribution of the survey. I also worked with the National Black Fellowship to assist in this endeavor.

Appreciative Inquiry Workshops

What is Appreciative Inquiry?

I determined to utilize appreciative inquiry (AI) for two workshops that would ensure that leaders addressing this issue recognize past strides while facing the reality of necessary changes. The process of AI addresses four questions:

1. What is? (Discovery) – Current A/G governance models

2. What could be? (Dream) – Opportunities for leadership from a social engagement context

3. What should be? (Design) – The principle of representative leadership

4. What will be? (Destiny) – Cultivation of new leadership opportunities

Due to the nature of my task at hand, I added "Defining" as a pre-step to the AI process, to examine the past and discuss the historic context of how we, as a movement, arrived at the "What is?" phase.

Logistical Preparations for the Workshop

I scheduled a session for June 2018 with the Great Lakes Regional Superintendents Cohort to conduct an appreciative inquiry workshop at their August 2018 retreat. This entailed requesting approval from Jeff Hlavin, superintendent of the Michigan District. In order to prepare for the workshop, I developed a pre-session report on the problem and opportunity of cultivating diverse leadership as well as an overview of the appreciative inquiry process. While my focus centered upon African American leaders, I did not address the transition toward a multiethnic congregation. Likewise, I did not deal with non-black minorities (e.g., East Indians, Native Americans, or Hispanics/Latinx). Also, I did not narrowly define the terms *black* or *African American* to the exclusion of black immigrants, whether new or historic. I also prepared handouts and a PowerPoint presentation for the workshops, which took approximately ninety minutes each.

The second workshop with the Great Lakes Regional Superintendents Cohort took place in August 2019 as a follow-up session to our 2018 designated action points.

Research Preparation for the Workshop

To prepare for the workshops, I first examined Scripture to gain insights on the principle of cultivation. I then turned my attention to the providence of God at work in promoting outsiders into positions of leadership. This demonstrated how such leaders release blessings and serve to advance the divine agenda while providing biblical justification for the cultivation of diverse leadership opportunities. I explored the narratives of several leaders in the Old Testament as those stories pertain to cultivating diverse leadership, including Joseph, the Hebrew slave promoted to prime minister in Egypt; Ruth, the Moabitess, the great-grandmother of King David; and Daniel, the teenager exiled into Babylon and promoted as a prophetic leader. As it pertains to representative leadership in the contemporary church, I also investigated the concept of tribal representation, in which the nation of Israel would appoint representatives by tribe to speak on behalf of the tribe in national matters.

My research in the New Testament focused on themes of inclusion and leadership, beginning with how Luke portrays the gospel as both for the marginalized and for all of humanity and every nation. The theme of representative leadership in the diaconate, the significance of the Antioch Church to diverse leadership, and the need for the Jerusalem Council were likewise explored. Special attention was given to diverse leadership as expressed through the empowered female leaders thriving in a patriarchal culture (Priscilla, Junia, and Phoebe). I concluded with a discussion on the Apostle John's vision of the nations as the bride of Christ in Revelation 5 and 14.

Another aspect of my research involved a review of key contemporary literature on the orthopraxy of cultivating leadership opportunities for African Americans. It began with an historical overview of the diverse beginnings of the modern Pentecostal movement and then briefly addressed current social challenges. Finally, I examined suggested models for building diverse and inclusive organizations.

Post-Workshop Interviews

Following the first workshop, I then conducted thirty-minute interviews in person with innovative Assemblies of God leaders who actively cultivate diverse leadership in their districts. The individuals included Duane Durst, superintendent, New York Ministry Network; Rich Guerra, superintendent, Southern California Ministry Network; Daniel Miller, superintendent, International Ministry Network; Brett Allen and Samuel Huddleston, superintendent and assistant superintendent, Northern California and Nevada Ministry Network and black executive presbyter (Huddleston).

Evaluation of the Workshops

Following the two workshops, interviews with the innovative leaders, and distribution of the survey, I objectively assessed the project to determine what proved effective and valuable for cultivating leadership opportunities for African Americans and what improvements need to be made for future implementations of the project.

Definition of Terms

The following definition of terms used throughout this book may prove helpful for clarification and information.

African Americans. People of color; black persons of African descent. This term is typically embraced by black Americans having familial roots that trace back to the North American slave trade. Likewise, the term is embraced by newer immigrant groups that self-identify as African American. The Assemblies of God Annual Church Ministries Report (ACMR) identifies within the Fellowship the following ethnic groups as black: African (misc.), Black (misc.), Caribbean (misc.), Ethiopian/Falasha, Ghanaian, Guyanese, Haitian, Jamaican, Malagasy, Nigerian, Somalian, and Trinidadian ethnic groups. The term African American remains interchangeable with *black*.[5]

Ethnic Fellowship/s. Currently, the Assemblies of God recognizes twenty-two ethnic fellowships. Based upon their size, these fellowships are granted representation at the AG General Presbytery. Typically, the fellowship president serves as a general presbyter. In the case of the National Black Fellowship, three executive officers serve as general presbyters.[6] The AG ethnic fellowships include the following:

- African AG Fellowship, USA
- Arabic Assemblies of God Fellowship, USA
- National Black Fellowship of the AG
- National Chinese Fellowship of the AG
- National Deaf Culture Fellowship of the AG
- Ethiopian Fellowship of the AG
- National Fijian Fellowship of the AG
- Filipino-American Christian Fellowship of the AG
- Ghanaian AG Fellowship, USA
- Haitian American Fellowship of the AG
- Hmong National Fellowship of the AG
- AG India Fellowship of America
- Indonesian Fellowship of the AG
- National Jewish Fellowship of the AG
- Native American Fellowship of the AG
- Nigerian Assemblies of God Fellowship, USA

- Romanian Alianta of the AG
- Southern Asian Fellowship of the AG
- US Tongan AG Fellowship
- Vietnamese Fellowship of the AG
- Japanese Fellowship of the Assemblies of God
- Caribbean Fellowship of the AG

Inclusive. Intentionally creating space for underrepresented groups so they may be engaged, involved, utilized, and valued.

Leadership Opportunities. Pathways for African Americans to serve in leadership roles at all levels within the Assemblies of God.

---

[1] Pew Research, "The Most and Least Racially Diverse U.S. Religious Groups," Pew Research, accessed June 11, 2018, https://www.pewresearch.org/fact-tank/2015/07/27/the-most-and-least-racially-diverse-u-s-religious-groups/ft_15-07-23_religiondiversityindex-1/.

[2] U.S. Census Bureau, "Population Race and Hispanic Report," U.S. Census Bureau, accessed June 11, 2108, https://www.census.gov/quickfacts/fact/table/US/PST045217.

[3] Pew Research, "The Most and Least Racially Diverse U.S. Religious Groups."

[4] The Great Lakes Regional cohort consists of superintendents from the following Assemblies of God districts: Ohio, Michigan, Indiana, Kentucky, Illinois, Appalachian, and the International Ministry Network. This regional cohort is representative of 1,330 churches totaling 157,669 members. General Council of the Assemblies of God, "2016 Full Statistical Report," General Secretary's Office, 2016, accessed June 12, 2018, https://ag.org/About/Statistics.

[5] General Council of the Assemblies of God, "2016 Race and Ethnicity Report," General Secretary's Office, June 6, 2017, accessed May 23, 2018, https://ag.org/About/Statistics.

[6] General Council of the Assemblies of God, "Language/Ethnic Fellowships," Office of Ethnic Relations, accessed May 23, 2018, http://ethnicrelations.ag.org/fellowships/

SECTION ONE:
Biblical Perspectives

Leaders must have the heart of God to accomplish His mission. The Scriptures declare a certain continuity about leadership. From God's first mandate offered to Adam and Eve to the leadership ethics of the Epistles, the Bible offers a value system that should govern the way people lead others. Indeed, the Word of God constrains biblical leaders to steward God's most precious resource—people.

The Scriptures serve as the primary resource for the formation of godly leaders. For example, the Book of Leviticus provides instructions for priests, while Moses declares that a king must provide for himself a personal, handwritten copy of the Law (Deut 17:18). Prophets hold kings and leaders to the standard of the Word (2 Chron 26:16). Christ admonishes His followers not to model their leadership in the manner of worldly rulers who "lord over" their followers (Luke 22:25). Instead, He instructs them to take up His example as a servant amongst them (vv. 26-27). The Apostle Paul affirms this model by declaring that the virtue of leaders remains greater than their gifting. In other words, biblically based leaders desire to please God. As a result, leaders should consistently evaluate their organizations and implement necessary change to align with God's will and honor His desires. Numerous scriptural models of godly leadership exist, and a study of these will reveal timeless principles that today's leaders must cultivate in managing an organization that honors God.

Section One will address the principle of biblical cultivation of leaders in Scripture in preparation for God's intervention and work

1

among His people. **Chapter 1** examines God's work in the Old Testament in the lives of Joseph, Ruth, Daniel, and tribal representatives who modeled leadership.

Chapter 2 discusses the biblical principle of cultivation as seen in terms of preparation for God's intervention in the New Testament. The chapter focuses on (1) the writings of Luke in terms of the gospel for the marginalized and all humanity, (2) empowered female leaders in Scripture who thrived in a patriarchal culture, and (3) the Apostle John's vision of the nations as a redeemed people.

God-honoring stewardship begins with cultivation. As illustrated by the creation narrative, which conveys the themes of responsibility and accountability, the concept of cultivation reflects God's heart for humanity.[1] The responsibility component alludes to leadership while accountability deals with stewardship. Genesis 1:28 declares that the Lord God "blessed them," affording both Adam and Eve a gift.[2] With this gift, however, came the function of oversight,[3] when God tells them to "fill the earth and subdue it" (v. 28).

Long before the Fall, God defines the relationship between creation and humanity. Through a sovereign declaration, He commands those created in His image "to be fruitful and multiply" (Gen 1:28). Further, not only does He command humanity to subdue and exert dominion over creation but also to cultivate and watch over the Garden (2:15). Initially, in the Garden, these directives comprise the creation mandate within a context of agrarian tools, fields, seeds, and livestock.[4] As humanity developed more complexity of existence, the timeless principle of cultivation has to be made relevant in every successive generation. God gives people what they need to steward the resources that He divinely supplies. This stewardship exists for the welfare of humanity, the good of creation, and the glory of the Lord.[5] Installed as the "rulers of creation," Adam and Even remain obligated to God for everything He mandates for them to steward and places under their leadership.[6] In effect, the Lord crowns humanity as royalty under His overarching authority; and as such, God tasks Adam and Eve to lead and manage creation.[7]

As the image bearers of the Lord, people have both the capacity to cultivate and create.[8] Genesis 2 sheds some insights on the function of leading and managing. The Scriptures declare that the Lord withheld rain from the Garden due to the lack of human presence to cultivate the ground: "… no bush of the field was yet in the land and no small plant of the field had yet sprung up—for the LORD God had not caused it to rain on the land, and there was no man to work the ground" (vv. 5-6). The Hebrew word for *cultivate* (`abad*) means "to work or serve,"[9] which conveys the necessity of human engagement and involvement. Genesis 2:6 infers a necessary partnership between the human effort of leadership and the Lord's blessing.[10] The ground stood ready to receive the influence of Adam and Eve as its first caretakers; the ground needed Adam's work to yield its fruitfulness. Likewise, God awaited Adam's leadership as well; He would release the rain under His sovereign control once Adam manifested human effort.[11] Human cultivation of the earth requires two distinct elements: heaven's rain and sunshine and the labor and care of humankind.[12]

When the first parents received the mandate from the Lord to exercise rulership over the earth, they also received spiritual authority from God. Prior to the Fall, they understood that no divide existed between the sacred and the secular, and God established Adam and Eve as stewards over all of creation.[13] As stewards, God empowered them with responsibility from Him and relationship with Him. This reflects the absence of a construct that delineated where human decision-making ends, and God's sovereignty begins, so cultivation of the earth requires invoking God's perspective in every decision.

As a minority group, blacks cannot ascend into leadership opportunities without the those who are in control cultivating spaces for them. These "cultivating leaders" are needed to create safe spaces where blacks can feel that their voices are valued, respected, and honored.

---

[1] K. A. Mathews, *Genesis 1-11:26,* vol. 1A of *The New American Commentary* (Nashville: Broadman & Holman Publishers, 1996), 175.

[2] All Scripture quotations, unless otherwise noted, are from the English Standard Version.

[3] Derek Kidner, *Genesis: An Introduction and Commentary,* vol. 1 of *Tyndale Old Testament Commentaries* (Downers Grove, IL: InterVarsity Press, 1967), 56.

[4] Mathews, *Genesis 1-11:26*, 175

[5] Ibid., 175.

[6] Franz Delitzsch and Carl Friedrich Keil, *Commentary on the Old Testament,* vol. 1 (Peabody, MA: Hendrickson, 1996), 41.

[7] William Messenger, *Theology of Work Project, Genesis through Revelation,* vol. 1 of *Theology of Work Bible Commentary* (Peabody, MA: Hendrickson Publishers, 2016), 11.

[8] K. A. Lyle et al., The Lexham Figurative Language of the New Testament Dataset, *Lexham Figurative Language of the Bible Glossary,* electronic ed. (Bellingham, WA: FaithLife 2016).

[9] Robert L. Thomas, *New American Standard Hebrew-Aramaic and Greek Dictionaries,* updated and electronic ed. (Anaheim, CA: Foundation Publications, 2016).

[10] Mathews, Gen 1-11:26, 193.

[11] Ibid.

[12] John Peter Lange, *A Commentary on the Holy Scriptures: Genesis* (Bellingham, WA: Logos Bible Software, 2008), 201.

[13] John C. Maxwell, "Why the Breakdown in the Line of Communication?" *The Maxwell Leadership Bible* (Nashville: Thomas Nelson, 2014), Gen. 3: 6-19n, loc 3909, Kindle.

1 The Biblical Principle of Cultivation: Preparing for God's Intervention in the Old Testament

Joseph's Appointment in Egypt

Joseph serves as a model of biblical leadership, one tempered by grace and meekness, full of authority and power, yet humble and godly. His promotion to vizier of Egypt does not merely bring him to a place of personal benefit but to a position of national servanthood, a position that ends up feeding an entire nation from carefully planned reserves.[1] Joseph presents a model of a leader given great power through the wise stewardship of human resources. In response, Joseph practices godly stewardship by using that power as a tool to care for others rather than as an instrument of tyranny. He uses his power and influence not only to save a nation but also his own family.[2]

Potiphar, and later Pharaoh, recognize Joseph, as an individual who possessed **five vital characteristics of leadership**: competence, capacity, intelligence, relational skills, and energy.[3] Joseph transitions through a series of placements and promotions, rising in rank in Potiphar's House (Gen 39:3-5), navigating prison (vv. 21-23), and ultimately being appointed vizier of Egypt by Pharaoh (41:41). Through Joseph's appointment, Pharaoh affirms these five leadership qualities. In Genesis 41:38-41, Pharaoh observes Joseph's **competence** in interpreting dreams, saying, "God has shown you these things" (v. 39). Second, he notes that Joseph has God's Spirit at work within him, which references Joseph's **capacity** (v. 38).

Pharaoh recognizes the supernatural gifting of prophetic foresight active in the life of Joseph. His observation bears witness to this capacity in the life of Joseph, a capacity demonstrated by Joseph's dreams in his youth (37:5, 9-10); by his being mocked as a dreamer by his brothers (v. 19); and by the first of his prison dreams (40:5, 8). Next, Pharaoh speaks of Joseph's **intelligence**, that he is both "wise and discreet" (v. 39). Pharaoh then affirms Joseph's **relational skills** by assigning him oversight of the people (v. 40). Finally, Pharaoh acknowledges the depths of Joseph's **energy** by declaring that, with the exception of himself, all will be ruled by Joseph's throne (v. 41).

Pharaoh uses his power to appoint Joseph to a position of leadership. Looking ahead to besetting times, the ruler of Egypt seeks someone with the requisite skillsets necessary to provide both vision and operational control over the challenges that the nation would face. Already in power, Pharaoh allocates the necessary space for an outsider to have influence and authority.[4] Though Pharaoh appoints a marginalized leader, he does not give Joseph this position as an act of tokenism, even though creating space for marginalized leaders often elicits protests advocating the avoidance of tokenism.

Pharaoh's objective does not include any hint of tokenism. Instead, he seeks to solve a serious threat facing the most powerful nation of Pharaoh's time. Further, Pharaoh does not hesitate to appoint Joseph, despite him being a Hebrew, a slave, and a prisoner in Egypt. Joseph proves equipped for the task, and Egypt's king cultivates the space for him to lead. The model Pharaoh sets forth goes far beyond mere toleration, too. Joseph receives real power to make significant decisions and to influence lasting change, both of which indicate that Pharaoh deeply appreciates what Joseph could bring to leadership:

> Appreciation is not toleration. When you tolerate someone (meaning you put up with or endure them), you dismiss that person as having little value to you or as someone who

doesn't make a significant contribution. To appreciate a person (meaning you recognize his quality, significance, or magnitude, or admire him greatly), you must make an intentional effort to see the very best in that individual. In this context, appreciating someone is not saying thank you, though that is important. It is seeing the value, worth, and quality in that individual.[5]

Pharaoh sees the intrinsic value of Joseph, and he willingly uses his power to appoint Joseph to leadership. He does it because Joseph is properly equipped and prepared for the challenge. Egypt's king gives Joseph the opportunity.

Like Egypt in Pharaoh's time, the United States faces unique challenges in a time of great change. Globalization has brought other nations into this nation. Such change requires questioning the effectiveness of old leadership models, especially within the Assemblies of God. Leaders at all levels of the Fellowship must question whether they adequately represent today's constituency. They must also self-regulate and make changes to cultivate opportunities. Finally, they must self-innovate, making necessary modifications to give marginalized leaders equal space to influence the organization.[6]

It should be noted that Pharaoh's promotion of Joseph was not an attempt to create diversity or to build an inclusive team. Rather, Joseph's promotion demonstrates that being a foreigner in Egypt did not hinder him from being a worthy candidate. The narrative also serves as an effective example of the use of power appointment, to promote a skilled and gifted individual into a place of leadership when current systems may not afford such opportunities.

Ruth's Relationship in Bethlehem

Another biblical character who serves as an example of the principle of cultivation in preparation for God's intervention is Ruth, after whom an entire book in the Bible is named. Along with her outgroup

7

status, Ruth had both integrity and commitment, and her story reminds leaders that wise stewardship requires abandoning the scarcity mindset.[7] Scarcity can create hopelessness and pull leaders into thinking that the best remains in the past or that missed moments of opportunity can never be redeemed. The Book of Ruth illustrates the power of God to redeem terrible situations. Ruth demonstrates a lesson on the providence of God, who works in the lives of individuals to establish His purposes.[8] On five occasions, the Book of Ruth refers to her as "Ruth the Moabitess," painting her as an outsider to Israel (1:22; 2:2; 2:21; 4:5; 4:10).[9] Ruth's status in Israel reflects that of a stranger, foreigner, and sojourner, yet she demonstrates how God takes those who begin in places of disadvantage and promotes them into places of significance. Ruth serves as a reminder of the heart of God to have a faith community reflective of every nation (Isa 56:7; Mark 11:17). She was reared by idolatrous people, yet she found significance and influence in Israel. Her story illustrates what happens when those who can empower others create space for an outsider to flourish.

The Character of Ruth

Compared to Ruth's Hebrew neighbors, disadvantage marked her Moabite heritage. Moab, a nation founded upon an indecent incestuous relationship between Lot and his daughters, developed their own theological hierarchy of deities (Gen 19:30-37). Chief among these was a god named Chemosh, to whom the Moabites likely offered human sacrifices (2 Kgs 3:27). The Moabite people engaged in battles against the nation of Israel (Judg 3:13-14; 1 Sam 22:3; 2 Sam 8:2; 2 Kgs 1:1; 13:20). Ruth would have had great difficulty finding peace and accommodation in Bethlehem, yet the narrative tells Ruth's story as one regarded for her worth as a person, not judged for her nationality nor her people's history or actions.[10] The text of Scripture makes implicit reference to Ruth's character.

In Ruth 1:16-18, Ruth's character is declared by the vow to Naomi when Ruth pledges fidelity to Naomi. The vow reflects her loyalty to Naomi, through four significant elements:

1. It was a vow of **covenant**: similar to the vow of marriage, it would only be broken by death.

2. It was a vow of a **commitment**: the vow speaks to the practical nature of living for each other.

3. It was a vow of **faith**: it recognized that the adoption of Naomi's faith would be the key to success.

4. It was a vow **made before God**: the vow invokes the name of God to serve as the overseer of the covenant. [11]

Likewise, Boaz affirms Ruth's loyalty to Naomi and speaks of Ruth as one of notable integrity (Ruth 2:11), noting how the Lord will reward her actions (v. 12). Ruth's character can also be extrapolated from her faithfulness in serving Naomi (vv. 2-3) and demonstrating submission to her mother-in-law's counsel (3:1-6). Ruth's conduct enables others to see the nature of God in her leadership.[12] Ruth did not rely on shallow charisma to accomplish God's work, something that today's leaders too often do: "Far too often we jump to mechanics, methods and techniques. We put style ahead of substance."[13] Ruth does not do this. Instead, she focuses on her internal values, ethics, and integrity, establishing a platform for future leadership and promotion in Bethlehem. Ruth remains focused on character.[14]

Ruth's Strategic Relationship

Ruth's character informs her strategic relationships. She demonstrates her work ethic in Boaz's field, which illustrates her fidelity to Naomi. Her ability to take coaching cues from Naomi ultimately gives way to her romance with Boaz. Ruth's relationships, while seemingly divinely orchestrated in origin, developed in part because of who she was as a person.

Ruth benefited from her relationship with her mother-in-law Naomi, a highly esteemed woman of Bethlehem (Ruth 1:19). Naomi helps Ruth navigate the cultural waters of this era in Israel (3:1-3). Naomi builds up credibility in Bethlehem as the community observes her journey from pain to restoration (4:15). Likewise, Ruth finds favor with Boaz. As a man of both influence and means (2:1), he invites Ruth to glean from his field (vv. 8-15). This act of compassion transforms into a relationship of intimacy, culminating in his redeeming of the house of Elimelech (4:9) and ultimately taking Ruth as his bride. Ruth goes from being a stranger and foreigner in Bethlehem to a great matriarch whom Scripture names in the genealogy of Jesus (Matt 1:15).

Ruth the Stranger

Boaz's initial treatment of Ruth demonstrates his honor of Ruth in obedience to the Law, which manifests in kindness, respect, and compassion. The Mosaic Law clearly commands the proper treatment of strangers. The Israelites were not to do wrong against the stranger (Exod 22:21), oppress the stranger (23:9), or prevent justice toward the stranger (Deut 24:17). Instead, the Law commands His people to treat the stranger as part of the community (23:16) and extend love toward them (Lev 19:18, 34).

The treatment of strangers in Israel served as an extension of their faith and demonstration of obedience to the God they served. The Lord wanted them to live with the conscious awareness that once they were strangers in Egypt and felt the hostility, ill-treatment, and ultimately enslavement at the hands of the Egyptians (Exod 22:21; 23:9). Further, it had been the loving intervention of the God of Israel that granted them supernatural deliverance from the chains of affliction (Deut 10:19).

10

Strangers of such treatment would experience justice, equity, fairness, and love and understand the distinct nature of Israel as a nation. The New Testament further reinforces the need to show love to strangers. This love motivates believers for evangelism (John 3:16), ethical interactions with others (13:35), and living as witnesses to the world (1 Cor 12:31).[15]

The Book of Ruth demonstrates how the minority stranger often needs the care and compassion of a well-established individual. Ruth benefits from the care of Naomi and the compassion of Boaz, who willingly create space for the minority. Such relationships, however, typically do not organically develop. Instead, these relationships require the insider to embrace the stranger and assist that person in finding success. The relationships must remain intentional and built upon trust, with the insider willing to leverage their power and influence on the behalf of the outsider. Such relationships cannot be focused on short-term gains but need to be nurtured over time.[16] At times, relationships with these dynamics at work can create feelings of inequity or obligatory demands. Both the insider and the outsider must strive to be invested and make the relationship mutually beneficial.[17]

Daniel's Influence in Babylon

A third biblical character who serves as an example of the principle of cultivation in preparation for God's intervention is the Hebrew nobleman Daniel (Dan 1:3, 6), taken into exile in Babylon under the rule of King Nebuchadnezzar. Though hardly a leader worth following in most respects, King Nebuchadnezzar did have some understanding of leadership potential. He had a process in place to recognize high-capacity individuals and set them apart for further development.[18] Daniel was endowed with a unique level of gifting that others recognized in him even in his youth. King Nebuchadnezzar identified Daniel and other similarly gifted, youthful peers and set them apart for further development in Babylon (Dan 1:4, 6,

17). Daniel's basic qualities appealed to the king, which models how leaders can cultivate leadership opportunities within their organizations, to find and grow potential leaders. The qualities of educational competence, intellectual prowess, and leadership aptitude remained readily observable in Daniel and his peers.[19] Because of this, Nebuchadnezzar recognized Daniel's potential. Given the opportunity to lead, Daniel exemplified how a person graced with natural giftings combined with personal growth, spiritual formation, and a commitment to excellence can flourish.

Daniel rose to prominence and influence after living in Babylon as a refugee under Nebuchadnezzar's captivity. Daniel arrived in Babylon as a youth and served under four kings throughout his lifetime. He stands as a model of high moral leadership—one never marred by poor choices or ethical failures. Likewise, he exemplifies a leader of integrity, demonstrating a lifelong commitment of fidelity to the Lord.[20] Hebrews 11 honors Daniel by mentioning him as a champion of faith with God "stopping the mouths of lions" (v. 33).

As Daniel transitions into the role of young prince, he displays developmental attributes that arise from both spiritual and character formation. A person of strong resolve, Daniel rejects foods that defile, and, with the Lord's help, he learns the wisdom and literature of Babylon (Dan 1:8, 17). The exponential growth he experiences demonstrates his immense capacity to learn, a trait that far exceeds that of his Babylonian peers (v. 20). Likewise, Daniel increases his prophetic sensitivity to interpret the dreams of the king (2:16), as well as his own ability to dream (7:1). Those who have great capacities for growth, whether through natural gifting, personal development, or supernatural means, often only need an opportunity to grow, such as provided by a leader who believes in them.

Daniel serves the rulers of Babylon with a mark of distinction. During his lifetime, the kingdom experiences a change of leadership three times: from Nebuchadnezzar to his son Belshazzar, then to

Darius the Mede, and finally, Cyrus the Persian. The Scriptures note that Nebuchadnezzar falls on his face to pay homage to Daniel and commands others to make an offering to Daniel (Dan 2:26). Belshazzar honors Daniel, making him third in line to the throne (5:29). Daniel also prospers under the rules of Darius and Cyrus (6:28). Valued by these leaders for his giftings and leadership abilities, Daniel never compromises his Hebrew identity. Instead, Daniel builds respect, rapport, and relationship with others.

Tribal Representatives
Model of Leading

The story of God commanding Moses to appoint leaders from every tribe is another example of leadership cultivation (Num 13). In preparation to take the land of promise, the Lord gives Moses the innovative leadership model, tribal representations (Exod 13). The Lord instructs him to appoint the chiefs (v. 2) of each tribe to serve as representatives in the endeavor. Moses notes that they were heads of the people of Israel, clearly an indication of leadership ability (v. 3). Often the default posture of emerging leaders is to construct teams with similar giftings. The implication that the Lord's instruction of obtaining leaders from every tribes would imply is, among other things, an attempt to cultivate leaders and build a team with a broad perspective.

Genesis 49 records the patriarch Jacob gathering his twelve sons and speaking prophetically into their lives individually. Notably, he speaks of their destiny, often using terms that point to future fulfillment (v. 2). This reflects the future development of identity, initially beginning as families, then clans, and ultimately tribes (Exod 1:5, 9, 12; 2:1). In Egypt, they experience two conflicting realities: the promise of the Abrahamic blessing that is to lead to growth, expansion, multiplication, and strength (1:7), and the oppression of enslavement at the hands of the Egyptians (1:7; 1:11). Exodus also reveals the sense of tribal identity among the Hebrews. The Scriptures first introduce Moses by declaring that his father belongs to the tribe of Levi (2:1), while describing Bezalel and the craftsmen of the tabernacle as belonging to the tribe of Judah (31:2), with Oholiab a part of the tribe of Dan (31:6).

The introductory narrative in the Book of Numbers emphasizes the importance of these identities as well. The Lord commands that the entire congregation of Israel be numbered by their tribal identities (1:2). As the Israelites depart from Egypt, the principle of tribal identity becomes deeply embedded in the Old Testament, as demonstrated by the twelve precious gemstones of the Urim and Thummim borne upon the high priest's breastplate (Exod 28:21, 30; 39:14) and the pillars established by Moses at the giving of the commands (24:4).[21] The value of tribal identity carries forth from the nation's primal formation under the leadership of Moses to Israel's national advancement under Joshua, when he commands the people to take twelve stones out of the Jordan (Josh 4:8). Valuing tribal identity becomes so ingrained in Israel that the prophet Elijah invokes tribal identity when he erects an altar to the Lord on Mount Carmel (1 Kgs 18:31).

Tribal identity also plays an important role in the story of Moses and the spies (Num 13).[22] God instructs Moses to send forth a representative of each tribe to investigate and evaluate the land (13:1).[23] Each tribe selects their own representative, a person regarded as a princely leader and head of the tribe, "recognized and trusted leaders believed to be equipped for the challenge" and persons of "wisdom and authority."[24]

John Calvin and Charles William Bingham posit that representative leadership conveys the following values:

1. **Creation of Credibility**: By each tribe being able to put forth their own witness, the suspicious nature of unilateral decision making was removed.

2. **Equity and Fairness**: The tribal appointments removed the feeling of marginalization that often accompanies those who are not adequately represented.

3. **Unity and Oneness**: With each tribe having an appointed leader, there was a sense that each part came together to represent the whole.

4. **Dignity and Honor**: Each tribe was able to self-identify their leader, which gave rise to each putting forth their best candidate.

5. **Shared Destiny**: Having a unified voice created the viewpoint that each tribe was determining the nation's future.[25]

Two of the tribal representatives, Caleb from the tribe of Judah (Num 13:6) and Joshua from the tribe of Ephraim (v. 8) report on the virtues of the land. They encourage the people to move forward and possess the land (v. 30; 14:6-7). The remainder of the peers operate in disbelief. Calvin and Bingham note that the narrative of Numbers 13 indicates a lack of faith in the response of the representatives. As with any leadership model, there exist both strengths and weakness, virtues and fragility, value and flaw.[26]

The Old Testament demonstrates through the examples of mentioned of just how vital the action of cultivating leadership opportunities for those who are outsiders. Often all a Joseph, Daniel, or Ruth need is for someone in power to open the door which in turn affords them the change to flourish; with the added benefit that as they succeed, the organization thrives as well!

---

[1] Carrie Sinclair Wolcott, "Joseph, Son of Jacob," in *The Lexham Bible Dictionary*,"

ed. John D. Barry et al. (Bellingham, WA: Lexham Press, 2016), Logos Bible Software.

[2] George W. Coats, "Joseph, Son of Jacob," in *The Anchor Yale Bible Dictionary*, ed. David Noel Freedman (New York: Doubleday, 1992), 976-981.

[3] Dan Reiland, *Amplified Leadership: 5 Practices to Establish Influence, Build People, and Impact Others for a Lifetime* (Lake Mary, FL: Charisma House, 2011), 1850, Kindle.

[4] A. Scott Moreau, Harold Netland, and Charles Van Engen, *Evangelical Dictionary of World Missions* (Grand Rapids, MI: Baker Books, 2000), 567.

[5] Troy Jones, *Recalibrate Your Church: How Your Church Can Reach Its Full Kingdom Impact* (Seattle: The Recalibrate Group, 2016), 28, Kindle.

[6] Moreau, Netland, Engen, *Evangelical Dictionary*, 567.

[7] Blue Letter Bible, "Ruth," *International Standard Bible Encyclopaedia*, Blue Letter Bible, last modified May 5, 2003, accessed July 6, 2019, https://www.blueletterbible.org/search/Dictionary/viewTopic.cfm.

[8] Ibid.

[9] Daniel Isaac Block, *Judges, Ruth*, vol. 6 of *The New American Commentary* (Nashville: Broadman & Holman Publishers, 1999), 588.

[10] H. Porter, "Moab; Moabites," *International Standard Bible Encyclopedia*, Blue Letter Bible, last modified May 5, 2003, accessed July 6, 2019, https://www.blueletterbible.org/search/Dictionary/viewTopic.cfm.

[11] Arthur E. Cundall and Leon Morris, *Judges and Ruth: An Introduction and Commentary*, vol. 7 of *Tyndale Old Testament Commentaries* (Downers Grove, IL: InterVarsity Press, 1968), 251; Block, *Judges, Ruth*, 643.

[12] John C. Maxwell, "God Honors Loyalty and Integrity," *The Maxwell Leadership Bible* (Nashville: Thomas Nelson, 2014), 18103, Kindle.

[13] Ibid.

[14] Ibid.

[15] R. K. Harrison, *Leviticus: An Introduction and Commentary*, vol. 3 of *Tyndale Old Testament Commentaries* (Downers Grove, IL: InterVarsity Press, 1980), 205.

[16] Scott Williams, *Church Diversity* (Green Forest, AR: New Leaf Publishing, 2011), 138.

[17] Christena Cleveland, *Disunity in Christ – Uncovering the Hidden Forces that Keep Us Apart*, (Downers Grove, IL: InterVarsity Press, 2013), 40.

[18] John C. Maxwell, "Leadership Qualification: Prerequisite for Responsibility," *The Maxwell Leadership Bible*, Dan. 1:4-19n, 65252, Kindle.

[19] René Péter-Contesse and John Ellington, *A Handbook on the Book of Daniel*, UBS Handbook Series (New York: United Bible Societies, 1994), 14.

[20] John C. Maxwell, "Profile in Leadership: Daniel: A Man Who Sought Understanding," *The Maxwell Leadership Bible*, Dan. 8:15, 17, 27n, 65479, Kindle.

[21] David Witthoff, ed., *The Lexham Cultural Ontology Glossary* (Bellingham, WA: Lexham Press, 2014). Blue Letter Bible, "Breastplate of the High Priest," *International Standard Bible Encyclopaedia*, Blue Letter Bible, last modified May 5, 2003, accessed July 6, 2019, https://www.blueletterbible.org/search/Dictionary/viewTopic.cfm.

[22] R. Dennis Cole, *Numbers*, vol. 3B of *The New American Commentary* (Nashville: Broadman & Holman Publishers, 2000), 217.

[23] John Peter Lange, *A Commentary on the Holy Scriptures: Numbers* (Bellingham, WA: Logos Bible Software, 2008), 72.

[24] Gerard Van Groningen, "Numbers," in *Evangelical Commentary on the Bible*, vol. 3 of *Baker Reference Library* (Grand Rapids, MI: Baker Book House, 1995), 93; John Wesley, *Explanatory Notes upon the Old Testament*, vol. 1 (Bristol: William Pine, 1765), 499.
[25] John Calvin and Charles William Bingham, *Commentaries on the Four Last Books of Moses Arranged in the Form of a Harmony*, vol. 4 (Bellingham, WA: Logos Bible Software, 2010), 55-56.
[26] Ibid.

2 The Biblical Principle of Cultivation: Preparing for God's Intervention in the New Testament

Introduction

The life and ministry of Jesus shifts the focus of narrative leadership opportunities from those demonstrated in Old Testament (where the Jewish outsider needed an advocate to create opportunities) to those demonstrated in the New Testament (where Jewish insiders needed to shift to a posture of cultivating leadership opportunities for Gentiles). This chapter will examine the Gospel of Luke and his concern for the disregarded, as well as the adaption of the faith from a Jewish focal point to a gospel for the nations.

Luke and the Gospel for the Marginalized

The inclusive nature of godly leadership permeates the New Testament, which focuses upon the leadership of Christ and of His disciples, as well as the cultivation of church leaders in the Early Church. The Apostle Luke's insights come from his professional training, experiences, and background. Paul describes his fellow disciple Luke as the "beloved physician" (Col 4:14), denoting a sense of camaraderie, intimacy, and friendship. As a physician, Luke utilizes language reflective of his training and craft. Further, he presents Jesus as a compassionate healer who willingly eases the suffering of those in pain.[1] Likewise, he highlights Jesus's concern for those without power or influence, such as the poor (Luke 14:13), women (8:48), and children (18:16).[2]

Luke demonstrates that regardless of how low one's social status may be, no person, including the poor, the leper, and the demonized, remains beyond the touch of Christ's love. Conversely, Luke demonstrates that even those in positions of influence and wealth, in society can realize the relevancy of Christ in their lives.[3] Luke writes his Gospel to fill the gaps in understanding experienced by the infant Church. Though early believers knew Christ, they needed more clarity, and Luke provides the needed information to present Him more fully.[4] Luke illustrates Christ as an approachable figure, inclusive of all, someone all could embrace. The narrative of Luke-Acts demonstrates Christ and His Church as a global phenomenon.[5]

Luke does not present Jesus as a new, sensational leader but as the fulfillment of the promised Messiah foretold in the Old Testament, who comes to fulfill God's promises first made to Abraham, the father of the faith. With a message of hope to humanity, Jesus prophetically connects the patriarchs to the present world.[6] The Synoptic Gospel writers each present Christ in an overarching theme that encapsulates both His message and ministry: Matthew defines Him with royalty, Mark as activity, John by His divine identity and Luke as love. In Luke's Gospel, this message of love extends in a unique fashion to people on the margins of society.[7]

Luke includes four of Jesus's parables that demonstrate His heart toward the marginalized. In them, the insignificant receive responsiveness, while God forsakes the powerful. Luke captures this theme spoken by the Virgin Mary in her Magnificat: "He has shown strength with his arm; he has scattered the proud in the thoughts of their hearts; he has brought down the mighty from their thrones and exalted those of humble estate; he has filled the hungry with good things, and the rich he has sent away empty" (Luke 1:51-53). Luke's Gospel illustrates how leaders, even minority ones, can appear from those in the margins of society.

Table 1: Parables Unique to Luke's Gospel Regarding the Marginalized[8]

Text	The Insignificant Protagonist	The Powerful Antagonist
Luke 10:29-37 The Parable of the Good Samaritan	The Samaritan who stopped and offered aid	The Priest, the Levite who did nothing
Luke 15:11-32 The Parable of the Prodigal Son	Disobedient son returns to be celebrated	Seemingly obedient son filled with contempt
Luke 16:19-31 – Parable of Rich Man and Lazarus	Lazarus comforted at Abraham's side	Rich man tormented in hell
Luke 18:1-8 Widow and Unjust Judge	Widow finds justice	Judge forced to respond
Luke 18:9-14 The Parable of The Pharisee and the Tax Collector	Tax collector justified by reflecting humility	The Pharisee is self-righteous and rejected because of pride.
Luke 18:9-14 Parable of Pharisee and Tax Collector	Humble man justified	Haughty man rejected

Luke illustrates this through recounting the witnessing of Christ's birth by the angels and lowly shepherds (Luke 2:15), the ministry of John the Baptist (3:3-20), the call of fishermen to become apostles (6:13), and the band of women who followed and funded the ministry of Christ (8:1-3), among others. Indeed, Luke makes a compelling argument for the cultivation of leaders who originate on the fringes of society. Often these individuals only need a strong leader who willingly calls them forth and takes a risk on them.

Acts: The Gospel for All Humanity

Every Nation Under Heaven

As first-century Jerusalem welcomed pilgrims to celebrate the Feast of Weeks (Heb., *Shavuot*), also known as Pentecost, a monumental event took place that forever altered the course of events for the world and the Church alike. The followers of Christ gathered, at His instruction, to await the promise of the Father, the baptism in the Holy Spirit (Acts 1:4). The Law instructs the Jewish people to observe and celebrate the feast (Exod 34:22), and Acts 2:5 notes that because of the pilgrimages to Jerusalem during *Shavuot*, Jerusalem at this time represents "every nation under heaven." Two distinct groups attend the festivities: those who had returned from the Jewish Diaspora to make the Holy City their home and those on a pilgrimage to participate in the feast but destined to return home.[9] Luke describes both groups as devout, indicating their religious piety and sincerity of faith: "Now there were staying in Jerusalem God-fearing Jews from every nation under heaven" (2:5).[10] The mention of these groups indicates that the scope of the events had implications of global significance. Though all were Jewish (including proselytes to Judaism), these individuals represented the nations and peoples of the world. Their presence spoke of humanity's need for a faith that would be for all people.[11]

In Acts 2:5, the Greek term Luke uses for "nations" is *ethnos*. This term frequently appears in the New Testament and generically refers to Gentiles or "a body of persons united by kinship, culture, and common traditions. In the plural it is frequently the group of non-Jews who become a central focus of the worldwide gospel proclamation."[12] Likewise, the word refers to people, a "nation of people," [13] "belonging to a people,"[14] or a "unit of people who make up a sociopolitical group and who share a presumed biological descent."[15]

Luke's use of *ethnos* reflects God's plans to work among the nations through the mission of the Church, sharing the gospel with all people, so they may be redeemed and adopted into the family of God. The Book of Acts reveals the expansion of this ethnos-centered approach, beginning with the conversation of Cornelius and the call of the Apostle Paul to the transition from the homogenous church in Jerusalem to the multiethnic congregation in Antioch.[16]

In Acts, God declares Paul as His chosen vessel sent to carry His name among the *ethnos* as well as the children of Israel (9:15), while Peter affirms God's work among the ethnos, noting that "God shows no partiality, but in every nation anyone who fears him and does what is right is acceptable to him" (10:35). Further, God pours His Spirit upon the Gentiles (10:45) and grants them repentance that leads to eternal life (11:38). Paul also affirms the apostolic ministry as a light to the Gentiles, which brings salvation to the ends of the earth (13:47-48).

Representative Leadership in the Diaconate

The vision Christ cast for the Church was that of a global movement. Christ mandated His followers to go to all nations and make disciples (Matt 28:19). His post-resurrection dialogue reinforces the Church as a global movement, declaring that the disciples would be witnesses to all the earth, first in Jerusalem and ultimately to the most remote places on earth (Acts 1:8).

As the Church begins to cultivate its own identity separate and distinct from that of Judaism, they begin in a unified, cohesive group (Acts 2:46); however, this unity faces its first challenge in Acts 6, with the feeding of the widows, as diversity begins to cause issues between two groups, the Hebrews and Hellenists. Both groups of converts shared Jewish roots, and now, as disciples who have accepted Christ as the promised Messiah (6:1), their differences were growing more apparent.[17]

The Hebrews in Acts 6 consisted of the Hebrew-speaking Jewish followers of Jesus, who lived in Jerusalem, while the Hellenist followers of Jesus in Acts 6 comprised people from the Greek-speaking world, such as Egypt, Syria, and Asia Minor, who also lived in Jerusalem.[18] The Hellenists likely formed various minority groups based upon their shared national and cultural identities.[19] The Hebrews did not ask or expect the Hellenists to abandon their cultural identities for the sake of acceptance by the Hebrews.

This has implications for leadership in today's church. Often seemingly well-meaning statements such as the affirmation of "color blindness" can ring hollow with those in a cultural minority who feel they must suppress cultural differences or avoid voicing input and insights that differ from their counterparts. This can lead to unintended consequences, such as hindering the benefits of the minority perspective and ultimately creating an organization that remains challenged in learning new perspectives, modifying to remain relevant, or growing in maturity.[20]

In Acts 6, the apostles summon the disciples to resolve the crisis of the Hellenists, who worried about their widows not receiving equity in the daily distribution of food (vv. 1-2). This lack of food threatened not only the widows but the larger community of the Hellenists. Because the widows did not have their basic needs met, the Hellenists likely would have felt that their safety and belonging remained at risk, such as described by Abraham Maslow's Hierarchy of Needs. This theory asserts that only when lower needs are met can a person begin to address their higher needs; if something violates lower needs, however, then they must address those threats in order to return to their current level of need:[21]

Table 2: Maslow's Hierarchy of Needs

Need Level	Category of Need	Type of Need	Traits
Level One	Physiological Needs	Biological	Food, Water, Rest, Warmth
Level Two	Safety Needs	Protective	Security, Stability, Order
Level Three	Esteem Needs	Belonging	Friendship, Community
Level Four	Self-Actualization	Fulfilment	Personal Success, Growth

The apostles understood the gravity of the situation and did not reject the claims by the Hellenists; instead, they listened carefully and offered a solution.

Through the wisdom of God and utilizing the gift of apostolic leadership, the apostles mitigate the threat by engaging all the disciples, advising them to self-appoint seven leaders who meet the criteria of having wisdom and a demonstrable Spirit-filled life (Acts 6:3). The invitation to involve the entire body fully engaged the disciples, which resulted in an agreeable solution that fell within the confines of the apostolic directives.[22] The number of disciples chosen to hold responsibility remains significant: the number seven "is an established designation. Local officials of the Jewish community and also ancient councils consisted of seven members."[23]

At times of organizational expansion, systems may fail under the stress. As the Early Church grew, its system for providing for the Hellenist widows had deteriorated. Rather than restraining the growth, however, the leaders of the infant Church chose to cultivate leadership opportunities. This decisive action of administration resolved the problem. The apostles and disciples did not view the system failure through a lens of annoyance. Rather, they accepted the responsibility and creatively addressed management issues by better stewarding the growth that the Lord had given them.[24]

The appointment of the seven in Acts 6:6 followed biblical models for creation of leadership opportunities. This echoes the patterns of leadership expansion demonstrated during Israel's formative years under Moses's leadership with the seventy elders (Num 11:16-25) and under Jethro's advice to select leaders to assist Moses (Exod 18:21-23). Jesus also created leadership opportunities with the appointment of the twelve apostles (Luke 6:13) and the seventy-two disciples (10:1), as did the Apostle Paul, who gave directive for the ministry of bishops, deacons, and other leaders (1 Tim 3; Titus 1). The Scriptures demonstrate that as needs arise, leaders select other leaders based upon a given set of criteria and then empower them to serve. A point of observation is that while they were all Jews, the selection of a team of Hellenist leaders to serve is not without consequence.[25] The shifting tides of change were beginning to shape the early infant Church. The ultimate vision of a movement among the nations, directed by teams of inclusive indigenousness leaders, started to form in the ethos of Church.

The Antioch Church

As Stephen, one of the first elected leaders, suffers martyrdom, persecution breaks out against the Jerusalem Church (Acts 8:1), forcing a scattering of the disciples from the Holy City into the surrounding areas. Luke chronicles the spread of the gospel from Jerusalem to Samaria by Philip (v. 6); as well, he records the conversion of the Ethiopian Eunuch (v. 27), the conversion of Saul and the inauguration of his ministry (Acts 9), and the conversion of Cornelius, the first Gentile to experience salvation in Christ and the baptism of the Holy Spirit (Acts 10). Gentiles, the *ethnos*, were coming to faith (11:1).

The first *intentional* evangelization of the Gentiles occurred, however, in Antioch, Greece.[26] Acts 11:20 notes that those leading the evangelistic thrust into Antioch were men from Cyprus and Cyrene. Historically, the island of Cyprus, prior to being named a Roman province in 58 B.C., was ruled and influenced by the Ptolemies of Egypt.[27] Likewise, Cyrene was a city strategically located in North Africa, which is modern day Libya.[28] As a point of observation, the first missional movement of the New Testament to the Gentiles of Antioch was led by those either influenced by or originating from the African continent.

For the first time, people *en masse* outside the Jewish faith heard the message of Christ. Antioch, a cosmopolitan city filled with ethnic diversity—Latins, Greeks, Jews, Asians, and Romans—served as a pivotal point for Christianity. The Jewish historian Josephus states that the city of Antioch was known as the "third city" of the Roman empire, only behind Rome and Alexandria in significance.[29]

At the time, the Jewish believers viewed the global nature of evangelism as a means to reach and call the people of the diaspora with the message that the Messianic hope found its fulfilment in Jesus Christ.[30] The Antioch Church, however, creates questions; it disrupts this perspective and the status quo as the movement of the gospel begins to bear fruit among Gentiles. The Antioch Church grows from a seedbed of evangelism and launches the Church into an international movement of mission. [31]

Questions Arise

The visitation of the grace of God to the Greeks of Antioch creates a new identity in the Church. The Greek Christians find salvation by grace through faith, which is found alone in Christ. They seemingly bypass the laws handed down through Judaism (Gal. 2:16). In response, the Jewish establishment questions the validity of the Greeks' conversion experiences. They question how the Greeks could be truly connected to Christ and to their patriarch Abraham without keeping the Law. They did not understand how these *ethne* could find acceptance and benefit from God's favor apart from adherence to the Law. The conversion of the believers at Antioch sent shock waves to Jerusalem.[32]

The beauty of the Antioch Church is reflected in the fact that it fully represents an inclusive community of Christian faith, where both Jews and Gentiles are united as one in Christ. The Church in Jerusalem was made up of Jews and proselytes (Acts 2:11, 41). As the message of faith spreads, key events occur that cultivate the opportunity of faith to come to the Gentiles. Like a musical crescendo, each event builds momentum. First is the dramatic conversion and call of Saul of Tarsus (Acts 9:1-9) whom the Lord declared to be a "chosen instrument" and whose calling is to "take [Jesus's] name to the Gentiles" (v. 15). Next, the conversion of Cornelius is led by the Apostle Peter (v. 45). Finally, is the testimony before the leaders in Jerusalem who, upon hearing Peter's accounting of events, determine that God has also granted life to the Gentiles (11:18).

Barnabas the Advocate

As the Lord moved in Antioch, leaders begin to emerge, demonstrating that the Church must cultivate space for empowered leaders (Acts 13:1).[33] Barnabas acted as a bridge for the Antioch Church, "a person serving to authenticate the Gentile witness at Antioch."[34] An individual known for high character and spiritual insight (11:24), Barnabas affirms the legitimacy of the work of the gospel in Antioch and engages the ministry of the Apostle Paul, launching him into his apostolic ministry to the *ethnos* (vv. 25-26). Antioch does not end the gospel proclamation of the Messiah to the Jewish people. Rather, the city serves as a starting point for the proclamation of the gospel to the nations—Jesus is the Savior of all people.[35]

The Need for the Jerusalem Council

The gospel rapidly spreads among the Gentiles, starting in Antioch (Acts 11:19-26), followed by the thrust of missional moves in Cyprus and Pisidian Antioch (Acts 13) as well as Iconium, Lystra, and Syria (Acts 14).[36] Under the power of the Holy Spirit and the supernatural calling of Barnabas and Saul, the gospel gains traction and bears fruit as they work among Gentiles (13:2). Still, a question looms over their work. They need to find resolution between the grace of Christ and the Law of Moses because some of the Judean leaders are teaching that salvation requires circumcision (15:1, 5).[37] As a result, the Jerusalem Council convenes to add clarity and direction for the Christian faith.

A significant point in Christianity for every generation to follow came in the form of the Jerusalem Council. The Council culminated from "the struggle by the early church ... to understand itself."[38] It stands as both a record of antiquity and a modern testimonial; it helps resolve the tension between "separation and relationship, law and grace, works and faith, distance and nearness."[39] The Council answered questions concerning the relationship of Gentile converts to the Mosaic Law and what it means to be a person of faith, fully accepted by Christ and the Body.

Acts 15 does not record comprehensive details of the Council, but it documents how the Spirit moved and directed the group's resolution.[40] The letter communicating the decisions of the Council affirms the Spirit's presence in the proceedings with the declaration that it "seemed good to the Holy Spirit and to us...." (v. 28)[41] The Council addressed the critical bookends of the faith—unity and mission. It cleared the distractions and addressed the fundamental issues of who Christ accepts and how to receive that acceptance.[42]

The Council's Content

Not surprisingly, given the Apostle Peter's biases and struggles with the acceptance of Gentiles, the Council chose him to speak first (Acts 10, 11; 15:5-11). The Holy Spirit uses Peter's encounter with Cornelius to validate the idea that salvation remains available to Gentiles. The text implies that if *Peter* offered the first endorsement of Gentile salvation, the Gentile mission that was orchestrated by the Church at Antioch under the direction of Holy Spirit *must* be valid (Acts 13). [43]

Next, Barnabas and Saul also affirm the legitimacy of the salvation of Gentiles. Finally, James, who likely serves as the chair of the committee, offers insight from the Prophet Amos (Amos 9:11-12). He declares that salvation comes by means of grace rather than religious ritual and human effort, and he directs that a letter be drafted and disseminated among the Gentiles (Acts 15:23).[44]

Council Results

Contemporary readers of Acts may have trouble fully ascertaining the implications of the Council's decision, which, in effect, allowed Gentiles to be regarded and embraced in equality.[45] They willingly create a space of equality for the recognition of Gentiles as the people of God. The Council bridges the narrative of the Gospels to the Epistles and shifts the focus from Jerusalem to Antioch and from the leadership of Peter to that of Paul in proclaiming the gospel to the Gentiles.[46]

Empowered Female Leaders Thriving in a Patriarchal Culture

Ethnic and cultural differences do not pose as the only barriers to leadership by minorities; gender differences also play a role. Considering that the world's population is fifty percent female, still there is an absence of this ratio being reflected in leadership.[47] Thus, it remains important to examine the contributions and influence of women's leadership in the New Testament since women of all ethnicities experience barriers to leadership positions.

Luke and Women

Marvin Richardson Vincent describes Luke's writings as "the Gospel of Womanhood."[48] His portrayal of women in his writings stands in contrast to the world of the New Testament, in which society typically did not hold women in high regard. Women's status in biblical times ranked alongside those of children, the poor, and other marginalized individuals. Women lived lives of subjection and strictly defined roles with clear responsibilities. Luke's writing provides a platform for recognizing the worthiness of women. His platform creates a thread of honor for women who led in the Early Church.[49]

In his Gospel, Luke speaks of the motherhood of both Elizabeth and Mary, telling of the supernatural conceptions reminiscent of Israel's matriarch, Sarah (Luke 1 and 2). He demonstrates how women were both early supporters of the ministry of Christ as well as His disciples (8:1-3) and recipients of His miracles (widow of Nain 7:11-17 and the case of the bent woman, 13:10-17). Luke also portrays women as devoted to Christ, such as the sinful woman who anoints Jesus's feet (7:36-50) and the story of the widow's mite (21:1-4). Luke records Jesus highlighting women in parables, such as the widow and the unjust judge (18:1-8) and the parable of the lost coin (15:8-10). He observes the role played by women as witnesses of the Lord's passion (23:27) and as caretakers of His body (23:55-56). Notably, Luke also records them as being the first witnesses of His resurrection (24:10).[50]

In Acts, as Luke records the history of the infant church, he continues to highlight and honor the contribution of women. He notes the presence of women in the Upper Room (Acts 1:14) and as early converts (8:12) and sufferers of persecution (9:2). Luke also highlights Lydia, an influential and wealthy woman who was the first female Greek convert (16:14). He also takes care to mention the daughters of Philip who, as prophets, exemplified leadership of first century women (21:8-9). Luke, of course, is not the only New Testament writer to highlight women in leadership. Paul continues where Luke leaves off and commends women in the leadership of the Early Church.

Priscilla

Despite how Emperor Claudius's decision to expel the Jewish people from Rome created civil upheaval and forced a Jewish migration (Acts 18:2), the providence of the Lord continued. The decision caused the providential relocation of two of the pivotal leaders of the Early Church: Priscilla and Aquila.[51] Relocating to Corinth, the couple meet the Apostle Paul returning from his second missionary journey. They befriend one another and found commonality as tentmakers (Acts 18:2) or, specifically, leather works.[52] Priscilla and her husband took advantage of well-established trade routes to carry the gospel of Jesus wherever their travels took them.[53]

Priscilla and Aquilla likely had strong relationships with the believers in Corinth.[54] Paul calls them his "co-workers in Christ Jesus," which affirms them as colleagues in ministry and missionary work (Rom 16:3).[55] While in Ephesus, Priscilla and her husband led a church gathering in their home, which indicates their affluent status. [56] They seemed uniquely equipped to launch and oversee first-century house church gatherings.[57]

Paul's Respect for Priscilla's Leadership

Priscilla and her husband likely converted to Christianity under the ministry of Paul while in Corinth (Acts 18:1-3). A mutual fondness developed between them as Paul refers to Priscilla and Aquila as fellow workers of the gospel (Rom 16:3-4). They shared living space and spent time together in the marketplace. She and Aquila accompanied Paul as he conducted ministry in the city of Ephesus (Acts 18:19). They worked shoulder to shoulder with Paul, developing mutual trust and learning to depend upon one another's fidelity to the relationship.

Often cited as a proponent of strict limitations upon women in leadership, Paul's seemingly narrow prescriptions on women's roles within the local assembly appear to suppress their role in church leadership; however, such interpretations remain devoid of cultural context (1 Cor 14:34-35; 1 Tim 2:12). Paul affirmed Priscilla and the experiences they shared in ministry, which reveals his true heart toward women in leadership. Alan F. Johnson makes a strong observation about Paul's statement concerning Priscilla and Aquila risking their lives for him (Rom 16:4): "This counters some mythical views of Paul as an unlovable, awkward misogynist, for it is hard to imagine Priscilla risking her neck for someone who puts down women."[58] Indeed, Paul valued women in the leadership of the Early Church.

Priscilla's Role in Leadership

The New Testament always names both Priscilla and Aquila when referring to them as a couple. The mentioning of both names not only points to their marital status but also their partnership and shared identities as leaders. Notably, the Scriptures most often mention Priscilla's name first, rather than Aquila.[59] Various scholars offer different explanations for the unusual order of names: Priscilla was the first to receive salvation and experience the call to ministry and was the most outspoken and visible;[60] she may have been a woman of some social status, so Paul named her first out of respect;[61] the Christian community highly regarded her, so Paul naming her first did not detract from Aquila but showed respect to

Priscilla.[62] Obviously, such perspectives demonstrate biased perspectives among some commentators.

Priscilla profoundly demonstrated her understanding of the gospel and ability to lead when she and Aquila thoroughly taught Apollos, a person of high esteem, about Jesus (Acts 18:18-28). Known for his eloquence of speech, Apollos then went to Achaia and used his newfound understanding to vigorously debate the Jewish opponents and prove from Scripture that "Jesus was the Messiah" (vv. 27-28).

Phoebe

In a long list of greetings and salutations at the end of the Epistle to the Romans, Paul mentions Phoebe first (16:1-2). Though only ever mentioned in these two verses, this prominent recognition of Phoebe indicates the respect the Apostle Paul had for her as a noteworthy leader in the Church. The recognition may have also served to provide her a customary letter of recommendation to aid in building rapport: "It is generally assumed that this letter (Romans) was taken to Rome by Phoebe, these verses introducing her to the Christian community."[63] In this passage, Paul notes that Phoebe is not only a sister in the Lord but also a "diakonos" (διάκονος), a Greek word that translates to "servant" or as "deacon," a formal title of service in an official capacity. Paul commends her for her service.[64] Textual clues, however, do indicate that Phoebe ministered as a deacon.[65]

Deborah Gill notes that Phoebe was in fact the overseer of the local assembly. She observes that the word "diakonos" (διάκονος) appearing in the singular, was a formal and individual title referring to a leader or an overseer and closely acquainting to the modern title of pastor. Further, the plural of the word *diakoneo* (διακονέω) was used to address a group of deacons, regardless of gender.[66]

As the leader and servant of the church in Cenchrea, Phoebe likely had material wealth and social influence. She served as the leader of the congregation, its patron, and the Christian community within the city.[67] As a result, Paul urges the church to assist her in her business among them (16:2). He uses a term that speaks to her fidelity and standing, deeming her a patron (προστάτις) to himself and many others. This term speaks to the economic contributions she made as well as her willingness to utilize her influence for the good of the ministry.[68]

Junia the Apostle

The extensive greeting of notable individuals at the end of Romans also includes a greeting to Andronicus and Junia (16:7). Scholars have debated the order of these names and whether any relationship exists between the two. Some assert that Andronicus and Junia were a married couple engaging in ministry together, similar to Priscilla and Aquila. Others, however, highlight the fact that Junia is the only woman linked to apostleship. The usage of the word "apostle" ranges from its most simplistic meaning as "sent one" to the formal treatment of being an official title. Further, some have asserted that the name Junia is a shortened version of a masculine name; however, this claim developed during the medieval era when the idea of a female apostle would have been absurd, prompting scribes to alter her name to appear more masculine in Scripture.[69] Prior to this point, "most commentators, including many of the early church fathers, interpreted the Greek name as Junia, the name of a woman, until as late as the 13th century."[70] Further, Peter Lampe notes that "without exception, the Church Fathers in late antiquity identified Andronicus' partner in Romans 16:7 as a woman."[71] Therefore, one can safely conclude that Junia was, in fact, a female apostle.[72]

Paul refers to Junia as a "fellow" Jew and prisoner with him (Rom 16:7). In a sense, she was a prisoner of war with Paul since they ministered in a conflict zone involving opposing kingdoms; they had been captured behind "enemy lines." The Apostle Paul notes her reputation as an apostle (16:7), but debate exists whether others knew her as an apostle.[73] Lastly, Paul shares that Junia came to know Christ before his own conversion (v. 7). Though some within the Church marginalize Junia, as well as Phoebe and Pricilla, in their ministries because of their gender, the witness of the text clearly indicates her status as an apostle.[74]

Paul's recognition of Junia reflects the encouragement he gives to the Philippians: "I press on toward the goal for the prize of the upward call of God in Christ Jesus." (3:15). Junia lived in a world that did not know how to view her, but she decides to focus on the Lord rather than her environment. This brief reference by Paul indicates that Junia served as a first-century heroine, a woman who boldly accepts the call of Christ and takes up the mantle of leadership by fully submitting to the Lord's command.

The Apostle John's Vision of the Nations as a Redeemed People

The Book of Revelation remains a book of hope. Within a seemingly mythical tale of characters such as beasts, horsemen, a dragon, and the lamb, the story of hope exists for humanity. The story consists of new things—a new name (2:17), a new Jerusalem (3:12), a new song (5:9), and a new heaven and new earth (21:1). One of the final pronouncements of the enthroned, victorious Christ consists of a promise to make all things new (21:5). He who conquered death now banishes all foes and redeems creation from the curse it has long been condemned to abide.[75]

The words John the Revelator employ speak to "a quality which has never existed before."[76] The story of Christ remains nothing short of an epic saga. He makes all things new through His incarnation,

His miracles and message, His death, His resurrection, His glorified body, His forgiveness and reconciliation, His release of the Holy Spirit, and His function as High Priest making intercession.[77]

His redemptive work necessitates new things.[78] John documents in Revelation 5:6 that the heavenly host sings a new song. The Hebraic model of the new song typically celebrates some new aspect of the Lord's loving-kindness, aspects identified by reflection upon events in which the Lord delivers His people. The Israelites considered new songs the most noble of songs. Numerous new songs appear in the Book of Psalms, and they celebrate the Lord's faithfulness toward His people during times of danger or oppression by enemies.

Table 3. New Songs in the Psalms

Text	New Song and Deliverance
Ps. 33:3 - Sing to him a new song; play skillfully on the strings, with loud shouts.	Vs. 7 - He gathers the waters of the sea as a heap Vs. 10 - The LORD brings the counsel of the nations to nothing; he frustrates the plans of the peoples. Vs. 16, 17 - The king is not saved by his great army; a warrior is not delivered by his great strength. The war horse is a false hope for salvation, and by its great might it cannot rescue.
Ps. 40:3 - He put a new song in my mouth, a song of praise to our God. Many will see and fear, and put their trust in the LORD.	Vs. 1, 2 - To the choirmaster. A Psalm of David. I waited patiently for the LORD; he inclined to me and heard my cry. He drew me up from the pit of destruction, out of the miry bog, and set my feet upon a rock, making my steps secure.

Ps. 96:1 - Oh sing to the LORD a new song; sing to the LORD, all the earth!	Vs. 3 - Declare his glory among the nations, his marvelous works among all the peoples! Vs. 5 – For all the gods of the peoples are idols, but the LORD made the heavens.
Ps. 98:1 - Oh sing to the LORD a new song, for he has done marvelous things! His right hand and his holy arm have worked salvation for him.	Vs. 2, 3 - The LORD has made known his salvation; he has revealed his righteousness in the sight of the nations. He has remembered his steadfast love and faithfulness to the house of Israel. All the ends of the earth have seen the salvation of our God.
Ps. 144:9 - I will sing a new song to you, O God; upon a ten-stringed harp I will play to you.	Vs. 4 - Man is like a breath; his days are like a passing shadow. Vs. 6 - Flash forth the lightning and scatter them; send out your arrows and rout them! Vs. 7 - Stretch out your hand from on high; rescue me and deliver me from the many waters, from the hand of foreigners,

Like Revelation 5:9, a new song proclaimed by the Prophet Isaiah speaks to the promised future deliverance: "Behold, the former things have come to pass, and new things I now declare; before they spring forth I tell you of them. Sing to the LORD a new song, his praise from the ends of the earth" (Isa 42:9-10). The Israelites sing this in anticipation of the lovingkindness that the Lord will reveal. Like John's vision of a redeemed humanity, believers now sing a new song because of the salvation God brings to every tribe, language, people, and nation (Rev 5:9).[79]

The beginning of the new song in Revelation 5:9 acknowledges His worthiness: "You are worthy." The term "worthy" points to His royalty as the King and sovereign ruler. He does not simply rule a geographic location but rather reigns as King of all the earth. Jesus established this regality by shedding His blood and dying on the cross. He paid the ransom for humanity, purchasing them for God. Not a fable, redemption remains a reality that the redeemed can celebrate.[80]

John speaks of unity within diversity when he declares "they sang a new song" (Rev 5:9). "They" refers to every tribe, representatives of every language, people, and nation. The Kingdom vision of inclusion becomes realized in redemption. The promises tucked away in the Old Testament come to light in the transaction of redemption. On earth, the nation of Israel develops the unique identity of being the people of God. They believe in this identity so strongly, though, that they lose sight of the Lord's greater purpose to utilize them as witnesses to the surrounding nations.

The Old Testament demonstrates God's heart and His redemptive plan to save all humanity, reflecting the promise first given to Abraham. The universality of the nature of God's plan revealed in Revelation 5:9-10 is also described by the Prophet Daniel, who says, "And to him was given dominion and glory and a kingdom, that all peoples, nations, and languages should serve him; his dominion is an everlasting dominion, which shall not pass away, and his kingdom one that shall not be destroyed" (Dan 7:14). John echoes this same universality:

> And they sang a new song, saying, "Worthy are you to take the scroll and to open its seals, for you were slain, and by your blood you ransomed people for God from every tribe and language and people and nation, and you have made them a kingdom and priests to our God, and they shall reign on the earth" (Rev 5:9-10).

The Apostle John and the Prophet Daniel both speak of the following: (1) the Kingdom being obtained, (2) universality of the people who will reign, (3) the eternal nature of the reign, (4) the central role of the Messiah.[81] These twin verses demonstrate the thread of redemption as an inclusive event for all humanity.

Contrary to the Kingdom, however, the church in the United States has failed to implement the vision revealed by John: "For at least the past 150 years of American history, churches have managed racial and ethnic diversity by segregating it."[82] Race elicits a unique conversation in the American Church. An inclusive approach to church leadership cannot be implemented by over-simplified means nor through the absence of honest conversation. Thankfully, the United States Assemblies of God has been blessed to experience congregational inclusiveness and diversity that allows for celebration, the singing of a new song as it were, yet the absence of this same diversity in leadership should result in prophetic lament and determination to shift toward a vision of the Kingdom.

Conclusion to Section One

The responsibility to cultivate leadership opportunities lies with leaders. The testimony of both the Old and New Testaments as recounted here in chapters 1 and 2 demonstrates that God raises leaders from minority groups as well as the marginalized. The witness of Scripture displays how He often challenges the status quo by promoting outsiders into places of leadership. Given such opportunities, these leaders blessed those they served and assisted God in advancing His agenda for their generation. This has implications for today's church leadership as well. Outsiders benefit from those in power willing to leverage influence to create space for minority leaders to effectively serve the Church. Leaders must remain intentional to elevate the forgotten people, those often found lingering in the shadow of closed opportunities. Minority leaders will lift the organization to unprecedented success and usher in the move of God in this generation. The challenge of calibrating organizations and institutions around such biblical models can seem like a foreboding task. Often, it may require shifting models, changing methods, and embracing new ways. The tension of forming proper orthodoxy must likewise be met with correct orthopraxy. Declaration is often easier that implementation.

---

[1] A. T. Roberson, "Gospel of Luke," *International Standard Bible Encyclopaedia*, Blue Letter Bible, last modified May 5, 2003, accessed July 6, 2019, https://www.blueletterbible.org/search/Dictionary/viewTopic.cfm.
[2] Ibid.
[3] Ibid.
[4] I. Howard Marshall, *The Gospel of Luke: A Commentary on the Greek Text*, New International Greek Testament Commentary (Exeter: Paternoster Press, 1978), 40.
[5] Ibid.
[6] Robert H. Stein, *Luke*, vol. 24 of *The New American Commentary* (Nashville: Broadman & Holman Publishers, 1992), 40.

[7] Leon Morris, *Luke: An Introduction and Commentary*, vol. 3 of *Tyndale New Testament Commentaries* (Downers Grove, IL: InterVarsity Press, 1988), 18.

[8] Marvin Richardson Vincent, *Word Studies in the New Testament*, vol. 1 (New York: Charles Scribner's Sons, 1887), 248-249.

[9] Richard I. Pervo, *Acts: A Commentary on the Book of Acts*, ed. Harold W. Attridge, Hermeneia—a Critical and Historical Commentary on the Bible (Minneapolis, MN: Fortress Press, 2009), 65–66; John B. Polhill, *Acts*, vol. 26 of *The New American Commentary* (Nashville: Broadman & Holman Publishers, 1992), 101.

[10] Barclay Moon Newman and Eugene Albert Nida, *A Handbook on the Acts of the Apostles*, UBS Handbook Series (New York: United Bible Societies, 1972), 36.

[11] I. Howard Marshall, *Acts: An Introduction and Commentary*, vol. 5 of *Tyndale New Testament Commentaries* (Downers Grove, IL: InterVarsity Press, 1980), 75.

[12] Matthew Minard, "Gentiles," in *Lexham Theological Wordbook*, ed. Douglas Mangum et al., Lexham Bible Reference Series (Bellingham, WA: Lexham Press, 2014), Logos Bible Software.

[13] Thomas, *New American Standard Hebrew-Aramaic*, Logos Bible Software.

[14] Chad Chambers, "Gentiles," in *The Lexham Bible Dictionary*, ed. John D. Barry et al. (Bellingham, WA: Lexham Press, 2016), Logos Bible Software.

[15] Biblical Studies Press, *The NET Bible First Edition Notes* (Biblical Studies Press, 2006), Acts 3:25.

[16] John Peter Lange, *A Commentary on the Holy Scriptures: Acts* (Bellingham, WA: Logos Bible Software, 2008), 37.

[17] Marshall, *Acts*, 134.

[18] Lange, *A Commentary on the Holy Scriptures: Acts*, 103.

[19] Polhill, *Acts*, 179.

[20] Cleveland, *Disunity*, 165.

[21] Sam McLeod, "Maslow's Hierarchy of Needs," Simply Psychology, accessed July 6, 2019, https://www.simplypsychology.org/maslow.html.

[22] Polhill, *Acts*, 180.

[23] Hans Conzelmann, *Acts of the Apostles: A Commentary on the Acts of the Apostles*, ed. Eldon Jay Epp and Christopher R. Matthews, trans. James Limburg, A. Thomas Kraabel, and Donald H. Juel, Hermeneia—a Critical and Historical Commentary on the Bible (Philadelphia: Fortress Press, 1987), 45.

[24] Polhill, *Acts*, 178.

[25] Conzelmann, *Acts*, 45.

[26] William Barclay, *The Acts of the Apostles*, rev. and updated 3rd ed. (Louisville, KY: Westminster John Knox Press, 2003), 102.

[27] John McRay, "Cyprus (Place)," ed. David Noel Freedman, *The Anchor Yale Bible Dictionary* (New York: Doubleday, 1992), 1229.

[28] W. S. LaSor, "Cyrene," ed. Geoffrey W. Bromiley, *The International Standard Bible Encyclopedia, Revised* (Wm. B. Eerdmans, 1979-1988), 844.

[29] Flavius Josephus, *The Wars of the Jews*, trans. William Whiston (Salt Lake City, UT: The Gutenberg Project) III.2.4, accessed July 12, 2019, http://www.gutenberg.org/ebooks/2850.

[30] Charles Simeon, *Horae Homileticae: John XIII to Acts*, vol. 14 (London: Holdsworth and Ball, 1833), 390.

[31] John R. W. Stott, *The Message of Acts: The Spirit, the Church & the World*, The Bible Speaks Today (Downers Grove, IL: InterVarsity Press, 1994), 203.

[32] Simeon, *Horae Homileticae*, 391.

33 William J. Larkin Jr., *Acts*, vol. 5 of *The IVP New Testament Commentary Series* (Westmont, IL: IVP Academic, 1995), Acts 11:19.

34 Ibid.

35 Stott, *The Message of Acts*, 200-201.

36 F. F. Bruce, "Council, Jerusalem," in *New Bible Dictionary*, ed. D. R. W. Wood et al. (Downers Grove, IL: InterVarsity Press, 1996), 232.

37 Ibid., 233.

38 Walter A. Elwell and Barry J. Beitzel, "Jerusalem Council," in *Baker Encyclopedia of the Bible* (Grand Rapids, MI: Baker Book House, 1988), 1137.

39 Charles B. Cousar, "Jerusalem, Council of," in *The Anchor Yale Bible Dictionary* ed. David Noel Freedman (New York: Doubleday, 1992), 766.

40 Elwell and Beitzel, "Jerusalem Council," 1137.

41 Cousar, "Jerusalem, Council of," 767.

42 Ibid.

43 Ibid., 768.

44 Allen C. Myers, *The Eerdmans Bible Dictionary* (Grand Rapids, MI: Eerdmans, 1987), 67; Cousar, "Jerusalem, Council of," 768.

45 Elwell and Beitzel, "Jerusalem Council," 1137.

46 Cousar, "Jerusalem, Council of," 768.

47 The World Bank Report, "Female Population," United Nations Population Division's World Population Prospects: 2019 Revision, accessed September 23, 2019, https://data.worldbank.org/indicator/SP.POP.TOTL.FE.ZS

48 Vincent, *Word Studies*, 248-249.

49 Morris, *Luke*, 50-51.

50 Ibid.

51 Walter A. Elwell and Barry J. Beitzel, "Priscilla and Aquila," in *Baker Encyclopedia of the Bible* (Grand Rapids, MI: Baker Book House, 1988), 1765.

52 A. F. Walls, "Aquila and Prisca, Priscilla," in *New Bible Dictionary*, ed. D. R. W. Wood et al. (Downers Grove, IL: InterVarsity Press, 1996), 61.

53 Polhill, *Acts*, 383.

54 Alan F. Johnson, *1 Corinthians*, vol. 7, The IVP New Testament Commentary Series (Westmont, IL: IVP Academic, 2004), 319.

55 Robert Jewett and Roy David Kotansky, *Romans: A Commentary*, ed. Eldon Jay Epp, Hermeneia—a Critical and Historical Commentary on the Bible (Minneapolis, MN: Fortress Press, 2006), 957.

56 Johnson, *1 Corinthians*, vol. 7, 319.

57 Pervo, *Acts*, 451.

58 Johnson, *1 Corinthians,* 319.

59 Elwell and Beitzel, "Priscilla and Aquila," 1765.

60 Blue Letter Bible, "Aquila," *International Standard Bible Encyclopaedia*, Blue Letter Bible, last modified May 5, 2003, accessed July 6, 2019, https://www.blueletterbible.org/search/Dictionary/viewTopic.cfm.

61 Walls, "Aquila and Prisca, Priscilla," 61.

62 Polhill, *Acts*, 382.

63 S. F. Hunter, "Phoebe," in *The International Standard Bible Encyclopaedia,* ed. James Orr et al. (Chicago: The Howard-Severance Company, 1915), 2386; Ben Witherington III and Darlene Hyatt, *Paul's Letter to the Romans: A Socio-Rhetorical Commentary* (Grand Rapids, MI: Wm. B. Eerdmans Publishing Co., 2004), 382.

64 Blue Letter Bible, "G1249 – *diakonos*," *Strong's Greek Lexicon*, Blue Letter Bible,

accessed June 18, 2019,
https://www.blueletterbible.org//lang/lexicon/lexicon.cfm?Strongs=G1249&t=
ESV.

65 Jeffrey D. Miller, "What Can We Say about Phoebe?" *Priscilla Papers* 25, no. 2 (Spring 2011), accessed August 16, 2019,
https://www.cbeinternational.org/resources/article/priscilla-papers/what-can-we-say-about-phoebe.

66 Deborah Gill, Phone interview with Darnell Williams, Lima, Ohio, September 23, 2019.

67 Paul J. Achtemeier, "Phoebe," in *The HarperCollins Bible Dictionary*, ed. Mark Allan Powell, rev. and updated ed. (New York: HarperCollins, 2011), 801.

68 Ibid.

69 Walter A. Elwell and Philip Wesley Comfort, *Tyndale Bible Dictionary*, Tyndale Reference Library (Wheaton, IL: Tyndale House Publishers, 2001), 764.

70 Robert Jones, "Women in Church Leadership," in *The Lexham Bible Dictionary*, ed. John D. Barry et al. (Bellingham, WA: Lexham Press, 2016).

71 Peter Lampe, "Junias (Person)," in *The Anchor Yale Bible Dictionary*, ed. David Noel Freedman (New York: Doubleday, 1992), 1127.

72 Ibid.

73 F. F. Bruce, *Romans: An Introduction and Commentary*, vol. 6 of *Tyndale New Testament Commentaries* (Downers Grove, IL: InterVarsity Press, 1985), 272.

74 Allison Quient, "Junia: Outstanding among the Apostles," CBE International, accessed July 12, 2019, https://www.cbeinternational.org/blogs/junia-outstanding-among-apostles.

75 Jürgen Roloff, *A Continental Commentary: The Revelation of John* (Minneapolis, MN: Fortress Press, 1993), 80.

76 William Barclay, *The Revelation of John*, rev. and updated 3rd ed., vol. 1, *The New Daily Study Bible* (Louisville, KY; London: Westminster John Knox Press, 2004), 194.

77 William C. Weinrich, ed., *Revelation*, vol. XII, *Ancient Christian Commentary on Scripture: New Testament* (Downers Grove, IL: InterVarsity Press, 2005), 79.

78 G. K. Beale, *The Book of Revelation: A Commentary on the Greek Text*, New International Greek Testament Commentary (Grand Rapids, MI: Paternoster Press, 1999), 358.

79 A.T. Robertson, *Word Pictures in the New Testament* (Nashville, TN: Broadman Press, 1933), Rev 5:9.

80 Leon Morris, *Revelation: An Introduction and Commentary*, vol. 20 of *Tyndale New Testament Commentaries* (Downers Grove, IL: InterVarsity Press, 1987), 100.

81 Beale, *The Book of Revelation*, 361.

82 Mark DeYmaz, *Leading a Healthy Multi-Ethnic Church: Seven Common Challenges and How to Overcome Them*, Leadership Network Innovation Series (Grand Rapids, MI: Zondervan, 2010), 15.

SECTION TWO:
Historic and Cultural Perspectives

At the turn of the twentieth century, Charles H. Duell, commissioner of the United States Patent and Trademark office, boldly asserted, "Everything that can be invented already has been invented."[1] In other words, Duell felt comfortable with the status quo, ignoring the possibility that life could improve through as-of-yet-unimagined inventions. This notion that society had already achieved its best reflected a sense of arrogance in what had already been achieved rather than a sense of humility in acknowledging what needed to change and improve.

In the context of church leadership, leaders must not make the same mistake as Duell in feeling content with the status quo. Church leaders remain under the injunction to constantly shape their organizations and people toward what Henry Blackaby appropriately calls "God's Agenda."[2] As it pertains to the issue of diversity and inclusion, leaders must step back and objectively wrestle with the grand question of how the collective actions of their community affect those within and outside their organizations.[3] They must look for troubling signs of contentment with the status quo and work toward a vision of a truly inclusive multiethnic church. As the church naturally gravitates toward the status quo, leaders must summon the requisite courage to fight against the assault of entropy that continually threatens organizations.[4]

Further, church leaders in the United States must ensure the Church remains relevant to an increasingly diverse society: "Organizations that once enjoyed the simplistic nature of homogeneity now find themselves wrestling with managing a new complexity, multiethnicity."[5] Though the Assemblies of God (AG) can directly trace its roots back to the Azusa Street Revival, a Pentecostal outpouring fathered by a black pastor, William J. Seymour, the AG grew ethnically homogenous over time and now finds itself wrestling with issues pertaining to a lack of ethnic diversity among its leaders. Organizationally, the Fellowship must remember its founding roots and remain guided by the *missio Dei* as it faces a changing world and asks how to adapt to the current landscape by cultivating opportunities for its underrepresented minority constituency.[6]

This section recounts the diverse and inclusive roots of American Pentecostalism, describes the current racial landscape of the Assemblies of God, and provides a brief overview of race in the United States. The final chapter describes how the Church can address racial integration and reconciliation in order to assist in the process of cultivating pathways to leadership for African Americans in the Assemblies of God.

---

[1] David J. Katz, "Everything That Can Be Invented Has Been Invented," Medium, July 4, 2015, accessed September 16, 2019, https://medium.com/swlh/everything-that-can-be-invented-has-been-invented-49c4376f548b.

[2] Henry Blackaby, *Spiritual Leadership* (Nashville, TN: B & H Publishing Group, 2006), 20.

[3] Christina Cleveland, *Disunity in Christ: Uncovering the Hidden Forces That Keep Us Apart* (Downers Grove, IL: IVP, 2013), 168-169.

[4] K. M. Lattea, "Leadership," in *Baker Encyclopedia of Psychology and Counseling*, 2nd ed., ed. D. G. Benner and P. C. Hill (Grand Rapids, MI: Baker Books, 1999), 676.

[5] A. Scott Moreau, H. Netland, C. van Engen, "Leadership," in *Evangelical Dictionary of World Missions* (Grand Rapids, MI: Baker Books, 2000), 567.

[6] Ibid.

3 The Diverse and Inclusive Roots of American Pentecostalism

Often to make sense of the present, a look to the past is needed. This looking back enables one to make sense of current realities as well as empowering decision for the future. A unique reality for American Pentecostals is the rich history of diversity demonstrated early in the movement's history.

The United States entered the turn of the twentieth century as a perplexed nation.[1] Hobbling forward from a bloody civil war that occurred nearly a generation earlier, coupled with the shift toward industrialization and the dying embers of Reconstruction, the nation was searching for an identity.[2] This era marked one of the low points of the country in terms of race relations. Myths of white racial superiority began dressing in the garb of scientific truth, yet underneath the fictional attire were only the rags of prejudice and racism.[3]

Despite rampant racism, pockets of progressive cities with diverse communities had developed; Los Angeles represented such a city. When William J. Seymour arrived in Los Angeles in 1906, he discovered a multi-ethnic, socio-economically diverse city. Not only did he find blacks and whites but also first-generation immigrants from countries around the world. A metropolis of 250,000 individuals, Los Angeles appeared as a vibrant microcosm of the entire world.[4] Still, in this diverse environment, a lack of integration remained pervasive. Not only did languages and ethnic groups separate people from each other, but churches also mirrored the heavy segregation of the wider community.[5]

47

In contrast, the Azusa Street Mission, the birthplace of Pentecostal revival, reflected the distinctive makeup of the city without the segregation: "The Azusa Mission with the power of the Spirit was crafting a new and radically inclusive community in which [hu]man-made barriers were erased."[6] The mission provided "a foretaste of the kingdom of God."[7] Frank Bartleman, an eyewitness of the Azusa Street Revival, documented the event, describing how "the color line was washed out by the blood."[8] Bartleman notes that the revival removed race from the individual's identity: "They simply referenced each other only as brother or sister, that was it; never was there the mention of color."[9] An openness to the Spirit had replaced the racism in hearts.

Behind this revival stood William J. Seymour, one of the venerated leaders of Pentecostalism in America.[10] On the surface, God's choice of Seymour to lead the revival may have seemed questionable to some. Blind in one eye and a minimally educated son of slaves, Seymour prayed for God to unleash Pentecost in the United States. In 1902, a few years before the revival, Seymour had ventured to Cincinnati, Ohio. There, Daniel Warner and his followers, known as Evening Light Saints, preached a radical form of racial equality and reconciliation. Their acceptance, inclusion, and teachings of equality profoundly shaped Seymour. He received training in their institute, where they treated him as a true brother in Christ. The Evening Light Saints testified that "we are saved and sanctified and not a drop of prejudice is in our hearts."[11] They credentialed Seymour, sending him forth as an Evening Light Minister.[12]

As a pastor in Los Angeles, Seymour sought to preserve the inclusive nature of the Azusa Street Mission. He firmly and unapologetically believed that Azusa provided the modern fulfillment of the prophecy of Joel 2:28-29, in which the Spirit's distinctive outpouring would break human-made barriers.[13] His beliefs about the outpouring of the Holy Spirit were influenced by Charles Parham, leader of a Bible school in Topeka, Kansas.[14]

Parham had hired for his children a black governess, Lucy Farrow, who eventually invited Seymour to Topeka and suggested he should attend Parham's school and learn from him, though Parham was a strict segregationist.[15] Though Parham believed that God could move upon blacks, he held a strong conviction that races should not co-mingle. Seymour enrolled as a student only to discover that his place of learning would not occur in the classroom with the other students but in the hallway. Seymour seized the moment, however, by demonstrating a thirst for knowledge and listening intently to every word of his newfound teacher. Parham postulated the theology that speaking in tongues represents the initial physical evidence of baptism in the Holy Spirit.[16]

This learning experience in Topeka, along with Seymour's heritage as the son of slaves and his exposure to the Evening Lights Saints Movement, provided him a distinctive and much-needed leadership opportunity at the Azusa Street Mission. No longer segregated out in the hall from peers in his Bible class, Seymour now served as leader of the first fully-integrated Pentecostal congregation. He remained so passionate about maintaining the inclusiveness of the mission that Seymour would often break up clusters of groups that seemed to pool together around racial identity.[17]

Sadly, however, the strong gravitational pull of the era's culture eventually proved overwhelming, fracturing the mission along racial lines. While it did attract high-capacity leaders who later went on to lead movements originating from Azusa Street, such as C. H. Mason and the Church of God in Christ, A. J. Tomlinson and the Church of God, as well as the founders of the Assemblies of God, the vision of multiethnic ministry with diverse leadership began to dim.[18]

Thankfully the deep roots of racial and ethnic inclusion are still producing fruit in the Assemblies of God. The promise the Spirit moving upon all flesh is a living reality (Joel 2:28). The mountain of challenge standing before us is the question of how the organization will adapt to such a move.

---

[1] This section, "The Diverse and Inclusive Roots of American Pentecostalism," is adapted from Darnell Williams, "William J. Seymour, Hero of the Faith," PTH 939: Church Revitalization and Revivals, Assemblies of God Theological Seminary, April 2018.

[2] Rufus Sanders, *William Joseph Seymour: Black Father of the 20th Century Pentecostal/Charismatic Movement* (Sandusky, OH: Alexandria Publications, 2003), 51.

[3] Joe Newman, *Race and the Assemblies of God: The Journey from Azusa Street to the Miracle of Memphis* (Youngstown, NY: Cambria Press, 2007), 8.

[4] Sanders, *William Joseph Seymour,* 80.

[5] Newman, *Race and the Assemblies of God,* 2.

[6] Gastón Espinosa, *William J. Seymour and the Origins of Global Pentecostalism: A Biography and Documentary History* (Durham, NC: Duke University Press, 2014), 1, xvi.

[7] Ibid.

[8] Frank Bartleman, *How Pentecost Came to Los Angeles: The Story Behind the Azusa Street Revival* (Springfield, MO: Gospel Publishing House, 2017), 13.

[9] Tommy Welchel and Michelle P. Griffith, *True Stories of the Miracles of Azusa Street and Beyond: Re-Live One of the Greatest Outpourings in History That Is Breaking Loose Once Again* (Shippensburg, PA: Destiny Image Publishing, 2013), 45.

[10] Larry Martin, *The Words That Changed the World … Azusa Street Sermons: William J. Seymour* vol. 5 of The Complete Azusa Street Library (Houston, TX: Christian Life Books, 1999), 9.

[11] Sanders, *William Joseph Seymour,* 54.

[12] Ibid.

[13] Ibid, 32.

[14] William Seymour, *The Great Azusa Street Revival: The Life and Sermons of William Seymour* (Fort Lauderdale, FL: Wilmington Publishing Group, 2006), 11.

[15] Newman, *Race and the Assemblies of God,* 47.

[16] Espinosa, *William J. Seymour,* 45.

[17] Welchel, *True Stories,* 2.

[18] Espinosa, *William J. Seymour,* 37.

4 The Current Racial Landscape of the Assemblies of God

Though predominantly white since the inception of the U.S. Assemblies of God in 1914, churches within the Fellowship now reflect much of the diversity of contemporary America, with over 35 percent of the Fellowship's churches self-identifying as non-white.[1] The Assemblies of God has experienced growth largely from Black and Latinx churches due to intentional outreach evangelism; also, some of the traditionally white congregations are now experiencing ethnic diversification.[2] This diversity now reaches into the highest offices of leadership within the Fellowship; as of 2019, minority leaders and women now comprise 40 percent of the Executive Presbytery.

Table 4: Executive Leadership Team and Executive Presbytery Minority/ Female Leadership[3]

Name	Ethnicity	Area of Service	Time of Service
John Maracle	Native American	Ethnic Fellowship Executive Presbyter	2007 – Current
Zollie Smith[4]	Black	Executive Director of U.S. Missions	2007 – 2017
Elizabeth ("Beth") Grant	White Female	Ordained Female Executive Presbyter	2009 – Current
Daniel De Leon	Hispanic	West Spanish Executive Presbyter	2017 – Current
Melissa Alfaro	Hispanic	Ordained Under 40 Executive Presbyter	2017 – Current

Malcolm Burleigh	Black	Executive Director of U.S. Missions	2017 - Current
Samuel Huddleston[5]	Black	Ordained African American Executive Presbyter	2017 – Current
Donna Barrett[6]	White Female	General Secretary	2018 – Current
Darnell Williams[7]	Black	Language Area – Other	2019 – Current

Despite these strides toward increasing diversity within churches, the Executive Leadership Team, and the Executive Presbytery, black leaders remain markedly absent at the district level, with the exception of two African American district leaders, Samuel Huddleston, assistant superintendent of the Northern California and Nevada District, and Darnell Williams, secretary/treasurer of the International Ministry Network. The diversity reflected in the Executive Presbytery did not happen organically. It came about with intentional and strategic moves that led to the creation of leadership opportunities for underrepresented groups. Often what the Spirit accomplishes organically will inevitably require human organization. My mentor, Bishop Burton Ross, would often remark, "Plan like there is no Spirit; then let the Spirit move like there is no plan."

---

[1] Assemblies of God, *Annual Church Ministries Report*, "Race and Ethnicity of AG U.S. Churches, 2016," General Secretary's Office, Assemblies of God, June 6, 2017, accessed September 29, 2019, https://ag.org/About/Statistics.
[2] Religious New Service, "Assemblies of God Highlights Value of Diversity for 100-Year Anniversary," *Huffington Post*, August 8, 2014, accessed September 18, 2019, https://www.huffpost.com/entry/assemblies-of-god-diversity.
[3] Assemblies of God, *Executive Presbytery*, "Our Non-Resident Executive Presbytery," Assemblies of God, accessed October 8, 2019, https://ag.org/About/Leadership-Team/Executive-Presbytery.
[4] John Kennedy, "Ready for His Next Assignment," *PE News*, February 13, 2017, accessed September 18, 2019, https://news.ag.org/news/ready-for-his-next-assignment.
[5] John Kennedy, "First Designated African American Executive Presbyter Elected," *PE News*, August 10, 2017, accessed September 18, 2019,

https://news.ag.org/en/News/First-Designated-African American-Executive-Presbyter-Elected.

[6] John Kennedy, "Groundbreaking Vote," *PE News,* August 2, 2019, accessed September 18, 2019, https://news.ag.org/News/Groundbreaking-Vote.

[7] John Kennedy, "New Executive Presbyters Elected," *PE News*, August 4, 2019, accessed September 18, 2019, https://news.ag.org/en/News/New-Executive-Presbyters-Elected.

5 Race in the United States

"The blues is like having the flu in your feelings. Instead of your nose being stuffed up, it's your heart that needs blowing"[1]

The perplexing issue of race in the United States serves as a reminder of the nation's painful past as it pertains to the terrible injustices perpetrated against enslaved Africans, Reconstruction and the Black Codes, Jim Crow laws, and segregation, all of which continue to leave lingering chains that bind Americans to current issues of racism. A recent poll of white and black clergy reveals a telling example of the depth of racial issues that persist in the United States. When asked the question, "Overall, how would you rate the job performance of President Trump?" white clergy responded with an approval rating of 51 percent. Of those, 25 percent strongly approve, while 26 percent somewhat approve. Notably, 20 percent marked "not sure." Meanwhile, black clergy had an approval rating of only 4 percent, with 85 percent disapproving of his performance.[2] Such stark differences in perspective point to how far the issue of race impacts the faith community.

The Absent Conversation

Issues surrounding race in the United States run deeply, producing a dearth of necessary, healthy communication that can assist people in understanding the seemingly distant past and its lingering impact on today's society.[3] Just as thorny weeds can choke the life of a plant, as illustrated in Jesus's Parable of the Sower (Mark 4:7), thorns of implicit bias, inequality, and racism still appear in the nation's fertile ground of democracy. These weeds persist, smothering the civility, honesty, vulnerability, and transparency needed to make progress in racial relations. In this weed-filled garden of democracy, only the toxic residue of distrust and cynicism persist.

Hard conversations about racial issues remain elusive because they make people unconformable.[4] The Church needs these conversations so that, as Martin Luther King, Jr. famously states, "We must learn to live together as brothers or perish together as fools."[5] In some regard, people have learned to live together; however, a striking absence of unity persists, the kind of needed unity that King referred to as "brotherhood."

One of the challenges to having meaningful conversations stems from differences in perspective. The issue of slavery illustrates such differences. While most people agree with characterizing slavery as a horrific institution and a stain on America's past, white people tend to view it as a historic event, one viewed through the lens of a long, dark past. Black people, however, continue to feel the pain of slavery with its dehumanization, injustice, monetization of people, and the dismantling of family—issues that remain ever present. Blacks easily draw a continuous line between America's slave past and modern demonstrations of inequities.[6] Current issues such as mass incarceration, poverty, disparity of wealth, and gaps in health indicators all point back to the fruits of America's past relationship to slavery.

Broken Windows

In his book *Tipping Point: How Little Things Can Make a Big Difference*, Malcolm Gladwell references the criminological "broken windows" theory. Gladwell references a story that first appeared in the *Atlantic* in 1982.[7] He explains how the first broken and unfixed window in a neighborhood signals its decline. The theory asserts that a neglected environment signals a lack of care, concern, and oversight. This first sign of neglect then opens the door for other deteriorating behaviors such as dumping trash, parking abandoned vehicles, and graffiti.

Ultimately, the neighborhood declines, as does property values, turning the area into a haven for undesirable activities, drugs, and crime.[8]

Broken windows do not only exist in neighborhoods, however. They also exist in American institutions, which cast ripple effects that affect black communities as well, creating challenges in urban areas as well as rural ones populated by poor people of color. These problems exist in education, criminal justice, healthcare access, and personal health, banking and lending, and retailers, the results of which manifest in things like food deserts, lower test scores, higher rates of incarceration, obesity, and lack of wealth creation.

Educational Disparities

A graphic example of a broken societal institutional is that of education. In the State of Ohio, funding for local school districts comes directly from revenues generated from local real estate property tax revenues. As a result, districts with low property values receive less funds than wealthier districts, resulting in thousands of dollars in funding difference per student.[9] Low school funding in poor districts contributes to a diminished quality of education for children living in those communities.[10] The impact on students includes older, run down facilities inconducive to learning needs, less access to technology, and the removal of extracurricular activities such as music and sports—programs often linked to student engagement and success.

Mass Incarceration

In his book, *Just Mercy*, Bryan Stevenson notes how the "prison population has increased from 300,000 people in the early 1970s to 2.3 million people in 2014"[11] Likewise, he notes that "one in every fifteen people born in the United States in 2001 is expected to go to jail or prison; one in every three black male babies born in this century is expected to be incarcerated."[12] The issues contributing to this problem remain complex, but mass incarceration has taken and continues to take a severe toll on the black community in a number of ways. In an article entitled "The School to Prison Pipeline, Explained," the authors note that "especially for older students, trouble at school can lead to their first contact with the criminal justice system" as schools increasingly outsource discipline to law enforcement, an approach that disproportionately affects signify-cantly more black students.[13]

Food Deserts

Food deserts occur in communities where high household poverty rates reign, which also tend to be densely populated minority neighborhoods.[14] The USDA defines a food desert as a place where either 500 people or 33 percent of the population reside more than one mile from a supermarket or large scale grocery store, rendering them without access to "affordable fruits, vegetables, whole grains, low-fat milk, and other foods that make up a full range of a healthy diet."[15] As for profit businesses, grocery stores do not operate in these areas because their profit margins remain lower there than doing business in other areas.[16] Due to this lack of access to nutri-tious foods, residents within food deserts have to utilize high margin cost convenience stores or stores such as Dollar General, which lack fresh produce. The consequences of such inaccessibility remain significant. The absence of fresh produce results in increased consumption of processed foods, simple carbohydrates, and high sugar and high fat foods, which contribute to increased morbidity and mortality.

Banking and Lending

As a response to the New Deal's 1934 National Housing Act, America's banking industry began a practice called *redlining*, which discriminated against black communities. Though the National Housing Act intended to attract Americans toward homeownership, bankers developed a system of color-coding communities, as noted by Jamelle Bouie in "A Tax on Blackness," a practice that assisted banks in determining where loans would be approved:[17]

1. A green neighborhood was white, affluent, Anglo-Saxon, and appropriately Protestant.

2. Blue ones had less desirable whites—Jews, Irish, and Italians—but was stable and upwardly mobile.

3. Yellow had undesirable, often working-class, whites.

4. Red ones were predominantly black or Mexican, regardless of wealth or class.[18]

Banks underwrote the developing boom of suburban communities for white middle class families while deeming mortgages as too risky for communities of color sitting within redlined neighborhoods. This practice created what is now known as America's inner cities and produced lingering effects such as systemic poverty within black communities, lack of familial generational prosperity, and the rise of inner city predatory lending institutions (i.e. high rate check cashing stores, title loan, pawn shops, and high interest payday loans).[19]

Politics and Faith

The tension between politics and faith has become more strained than ever in the United States. Anger and animosity have created an environment that remains polarized and filled with distrust and cynicism.[20] Broadly speaking, evidence for these conditions appears everywhere, from the national news down to personal interactions on social media platforms. The nation seems stuck in a quagmire when it comes to politics. Sadly, the faith community often echoes the worldly voices of division rather than operating as a redemptive force. The ever-expanding liberalism of the Democratic Party and the absence of diversity within the Republican Party leaves many of today's believers feeling politically orphaned.[21]

The consequential presidential elections of both Barack Obama and Donald Trump have shaped much of the current landscape. Obama, celebrated as the nation's first African American president, was also politically liberal, making many white evangelicals nervous. This gave rise to Donald Trump, who sought to stem the tide of liberalism and represent anti-abortion, pro-Israel, anti-immigration conservatives. Within this landscape, evangelicals find themselves caught between two politically opposite approaches, neither of which satisfy biblical values. Evangelicals only add to the danger as they swap prophetic activity for contentment with their political parties, as illustrated by the research conducted by the Billy Graham Center:[22]

1. Two-thirds of evangelicals (67 percent) believe that "Christians can benefit from a political leader even if that leader's personal life does not line up with Christian teaching."

2. Seventy-five percent of evangelicals who identify as pro-life expressed a willingness to vote for a pro-life candidate regardless of political party.

3. Forty-three percent of evangelicals agreed with the statement "When a political leader is making important decisions I support, I should also support the leader when they say or do things I disagree with."

4. Evangelicals value politics more than non-evangelicals. Nearly one-third of evangelicals (30 percent) said politics is "extremely important," while only 18 percent of non-evangelicals judged it so, and nearly twice as many non-evangelicals (13 percent) said politics is "not very important" compared to 7 percent of evangelicals.[23]

Weighing in on the currently polarized political and racial environment, John C. Richards Jr. observes that the short-term gains of President Trump's conservatism will create a long-term vacuum of black engagement: "I fear evangelicals have risked years of process-ing past racial trauma for a future devoid of Black voices among them."[24] The Church must find its prophetic voice and lead the way as a redemptive force.

The American Church stands at a critical crossroad in addressing issues social engagement and biblical values. This tension of these two factors cannot be addressed with over simplified answers. It will take the deep of collaboration, margin for grace and posture of understanding to forge a pathway forward.

---

[1] Edward Gilbreath, *Reconciliation Blues: A Black Evangelical's Inside View of White Christianity* (Downers Grove, IL: InterVarsity Press 2006), 20, Kindle.

[2] Lifeway Research, "Half of Protestant Pastors Approve of Trump's Job Performance," Lifeway, October 11, 2018, accessed June 26, 2019, https://lifewayresearch.com/2018/10/11/half-of-protestant-pastors-approve-of-trumps-job-performance/accessed June 26, 2019.

[3] George Barna, *The Seven Faith Tribes: Who They Are, What They Believe, and Why They Matter* (Carol Stream, IL: Tyndale House Publishers, 2009), 1847, Kindle.

[4] Daniel Hill, *White Awake: An Honest Look at What It Means to Be White* (Downers Grove, IL: InterVarsity Press, 2017), 38.

[5] Martin Luther King Jr., in a speech given in St. Louis, MO, March 22, 1964, accessed June 30, 2019, https://borgenproject.org/martin-luther-king-jr-quotes-on-family/.

[6] Soong-Chan Rah, *Many Colors: Cultural Intelligence for a Changing Church* (Chicago: Moody Publishers, 2010), 48.

[7] James Wilson and George Kelling, "Broken Windows: The Police and Neighborhood Safety," *The Atlantic*, March 1982, accessed September 18, 2019, https://www.theatlantic.com/magazine/archive/1982/03/broken-windows/304465/.

[8] Malcolm Gladwell, *The Tipping Point: How Little Things Can Make a Big Difference*, audible ed. (New York: Little, Brown and Company, 2006), Audible.

[9] Darrel Rowland, "Ohio School Funding Plan Still Shortchanges Poor Districts Analysis Finds," *The Columbus Dispatch*, September 5, 2019, accessed September 10, 2019, https://www.dispatch.com/news/20190905/ohio-school-funding-plan-still-shortchanges-poor-districts-analysis-finds.

[10] Terry Smith, "Ohio's School Funding System Was Bad in 1997; It's Still Bad Today," *Athens News,* May 30, 2018, June 30, 2019, https://www.athensnews.com/opinion/wearing_thin/ohio-s-school-funding-system-was-bad-in-it-s/article_a16dc2e8-641a-11e8-9662-13c1a8a8f31f.html.

[11] Bryan Stevenson, *Just Mercy*, movie tie-in ed. (New York: Random House Publishing Group, 2014), 239, Kindle.

[12] Stevenson, *Just Mercy*, 242, Kindle.

[13] Dara Lind and Libby Nelson, "The School to Prison Pipeline, Explained," Justice Policy Institute, February 24, 2015, accessed September 19, 2019, http://www.justicepolicy.org/news/8775.

[14] Tulane University, "Food Deserts in America (Infographic)," Tulane University School of Social Work, May 10, 2018, accessed September 19, 2019, https://socialwork.tulane.edu/blog/food-deserts-in-america.

[15] United States Department of Agriculture, *Access to Affordable and Nutritious Food: Measuring and Understanding Food Deserts and Their Consequences*, Centers for Disease Control and Prevention August 21, 2017, accessed June 10, 2019, https://www.ers.usda.gov/webdocs/publications/42711/12716_ap036_1_.pdf?v=41055.

[16] Dave Green, "The Shocking Reality of Food Deserts in America," Feeding Children Everywhere, July 25, 2016, accessed September 19, 2019, https://www.feedingchildreneverywhere.com/blog/the-shocking-reality-of-food-deserts-in-america/.

[17] Terry Gross, "A Forgotten History of How the U.S. Government Segregated America," Fresh Air, National Public Radio, March 3, 2017, accessed June 20, 2019, https://www.npr.org/2017/05/03/526655831/a-forgotten-history-of-how-the-u-s-government-segregated-america.

[18] Jamelle Bouie, "A Tax on Blackness," *Slate*, May 13, 2015, accessed October 1, 2019, https://slate.com/news-and-politics/2015/05/racism-in-real-estate-landlords-redlining-housing-values-and-discrimination.html.

[19] Bouie, "A Tax on Blackness."

[20] Ed Stetzer, "Faith and Politics: Living the Golden Rule," *Christianity Today*, July 23, 2014, accessed June 20, 2019, https://www.christianitytoday.com/edstetzer/2014/july/faith-and-politics-living-golden-rule.html.

[21] John C. Richards, "For Blacks, Lies Matter: Black Christians, the Trump Presidency, and New Research," *Christianity Today*, October 18, 2018, accessed June 20, 2019, https://www.christianitytoday.com/edstetzer/2018/october/for-blacks-lies-matter-black-christians-trump-presidency-an.html.

[22] Gilbreath, *Reconciliation Blues*, 9, Kindle.

[23] Billy Graham Center, "Evangelicals More Issue Oriented Than Candidate Focused, New Data Shows," Wheaton College, October 18, 2018, accessed June 23, 2019, https://www.billygrahamcenter.com/wp-content/uploads/2018/10/Evangelical-Voting-Research.pdf.

[24] Richards, "For Blacks, Lies Matter."

Conclusion to Section Two

Section two addressed (chapter 3) the diverse and inclusive roots of American Pentecostalism, examined the current racial landscape of the Assemblies of God (chapter 4), and overviewed race in general in the United States (chapter 5).

Section three will articulate (in chapter 6) practical steps the Church can take (and specifically the AG) to address racial integration and reconciliation to meet the ever-growing realities and opportunities of our day. Chapter 7 provides teaching resources associated with my doctoral project that can be adapted for multiple ministry settings and provide a window into some of the complexities and exciting opportunities that lie ahead.

As you take on these challenges, however, it is important to keep in mind further research yet to do in reference to valuing the role of black leaders within the Church. Three areas of study may prove beneficial: the birth of the Antioch Church as described in Acts 11:19-30 regarding the missional thrust of the Early Church, traceable back to individuals residing in Cyprus and Cyrene, a city in present day Libya. Antioch subsequently came to represent the first expression of the body of Christ outside of Jerusalem, an example of the plan of the Lord for the nations. Deeper study of this could prove fascinating and meaningful.

Second, an historic review of the Azusa Street Revival through the lens of a multiethnic, diverse movement would offer valuable lessons for today's Church. American Pentecostalism traces its foundation back to this revival, one led by William Seymour, an African American son of slaves. Much like Antioch, Azusa provided a paradigm-shifting moment in the Church. Racial tensions, however, ultimately splintered the fruit of the revival into a number of racially homogeneous groups, many of which still struggle to recapture what they lost from Azusa. Deeper research and reflection on this past may reveal needed adjustments for today's Church.

Last, research should explore barriers to minority leadership within the Fellowship. The issue of diversity and inclusion will not go away as the nation has shifted into a new normal. Diversity now represents the status quo. Questions linger as to what barriers hinder the Assemblies of God from shifting into a more proactive posture for cultivating minority leadership opportunities. The field implementation of my doctoral project uncovered lingering questions about diverse leadership, which ultimately seem rooted in certain fears: "Will there be enough leadership positions to go around?" (fear stemming from a scarcity mindset); "Who will be in control?" (fear of governance); "What does diverse leadership mean for me and my church's wellbeing?" (fear of the unknown).

Research should explore the perspectives of those resistant to diverse leadership, so they may eventually come to understand that when diverse believers co-labor with the Lord (1 Cor. 3:19), they will innovatively cultivate the best of the organization.

SECTION THREE:
Practical Perspectives

As the previous chapters demonstrate, multiethnic leadership remains close to the heart of God. Embracing the mission of God requires the Church to embrace His inclusive nature. The Church must rebuke the racism, prejudice, bias, colorism, and overall disregard for the diversity found within His creation. It also must overcome the inaction, hesitation, and silence that continually threatens such rebukes.

As the Church works to embrace God's mission by becoming more inclusive, it must wed its orthodoxy to orthopraxy. The Church must take the practical steps necessary and available to align with its teaching. Within this imperative in mind, chapter 6 of this section presents ten specific principles to address racial integration and reconciliation to meet the ever-growing realities and opportunities of our day.

> "As the Church works to embrace God's mission by becoming more inclusive, it must wed its orthodoxy to orthopraxy."

Additional practical resources in this section include the material prepared for the field project for my doctoral work, which sought to walk out these principles through two appreciative inquiry (AI) workshops with the Great Lakes Superintendent Cohort of the Assemblies of God (AG) and a set of interviews with innovative leaders, designed to help cultivate and promote leadership opportunities for African Americans. This book's Introduction described the planning, implementation, and evaluation steps taken to carry out that project. Chapters 7 and 8 provide instructional information on the Appreciative Inquiry process, which you can adapt to your own ministry context in order to cultivate leadership opportunities for African Americans. Chapter 9 presents three sets of results related to the doctoral project: (a) results of the interviews I conducted with key innovative leaders, (b) results of the second workshop, and (c) results of the Black Credential Holders Survey.

6 How the Church Can Address Racial Integration and Reconciliation

As Martin Luther King once noted about the Church, "They tell me that there is more integration in the entertaining world and other secular agencies than there is in the Christian church. How appalling that is."[1] Just as the Church struggled in King's time to lead the way with racial integration, it continues to struggle in clarifying its mission in light of contemporary issues because "the very ground upon which the nation stands is shifting, from Christian to Post Christian; from modernity to post modernity; and from mono-ethnic identity to a multiethnic identity."[2] This current shift to a multiethnic identity provides a keen opportunity for the Church to lead. As the nation moves ever closer to an absence of a clearly defined racial majority, the Church as the body of Christ has increased opportunities to speak with messages of redemption and reconciliation. The over-simplistic approaches of yesteryear have failed to provide any lift above racial inequalities and push progress forward. It would be a tragedy for the Church in America to mismanage this moment.[3]

> "This current shift to a multiethnic identity provides a keen opportunity for the Church to lead."

This chapter discusses ten principles that pastors, Christian leaders, and churches can utilize in facilitating integration and reconciliation. At the end of the chapter are recommendations for Assemblies of God leaders for helping walk out these principles.

Clarify the Win

In navigating major issues such as racial integration and reconciliation within the Church, the authors of *Seven Practices of Effective Ministry* note the necessity of clarifying the win: "The church should be more determined than any other kind of organization to clarify the win simply because the stakes are so much higher: eternity hangs in the balance."[4] Clarifying the win, they rightfully argue, requires the development of a proper scorecard and recorded progress.[5] Thus, the Church must ask what a win looks like for racial issues.

Addressing racial issues provides the Church a prophetic witness to the world. In 1962, Everett Rodger developed his now famous Diffusion of Innovation curve. He noted that people tend to respond to innovations in waves of reaction, from the innovators, to the early adapters, followed by the early majority, then the late majority, and finally the laggards.[6] The Church in the United States has too often harbored laggards in dealing with issues such as biblical justice, racial inclusion, equality, and equity. Instead, it needs to remain on the forefront of biblical justice.

Exercise Your Prophetic Voice

The Church in the United States "has often times been guilty of whispering or whining rather than proclamation and pronouncement."[7] In contrast, the prophetic voice of the Church not only speaks up for morality, justice, and life, but it likewise speaks against inequity. The gospel of redemption is also the gospel of reconciliation. The salvation of souls remains as important as the lifting of lives. Destroying demonic yokes and dismantling oppressive systems work in tandem.[8] Pulling down oppressive systems does not require so much a social justice gospel as it does a redemptive gospel, a gospel willing to boldly face social issues.[9]

Church leaders often advise Christians to be apolitical to preserve and protect orthodoxy, yet this stance seems to lend itself to the art of cherry picking, in which Christians pick some issues to champion while avoiding others. Further, those issues that Christians often avoid seem to disproportionally impact minorities and those on the margins.[10] History has shown, however, that when churches stand up and make their voices heard, change happens. At times, such change has yielded significant results as demonstrated by the courageous leadership of Wilberforce, Bonhoeffer and King. More often, though, the changes happen on much smaller levels, in neighborhoods, communities, and other social pockets. There, change may come slowly but steadily, with the long view in mind.[11]

Challenge the Status Quo

Find the Right Time

Effectively cultivating multiethnicity within any organization does not come without both celebrations and seasons of consternation. Indeed, summoning the courage to challenge the successes of the status quo risks creating chaos, and doing the right thing requires a great deal of concerted effort. Still, such organizational change remains necessary. The only question to ask is when such change should come, according to leadership theorist Samuel Chand, who argues that change should happen during an organization's mature phase. Chand asserts that while others

> "Change should happen during an organization's mature phase."

within the organization enjoy the status quo when all is well, the leader understands that season as the right season to break the status quo to give birth to something new.[12] Breaking the status quo will result in a period of confusion in which the leader casts new vision while the organization questions it.[13] The leader must determine to stay the course because the disruption will bring new life to the organization (see figure below).[14] Without such life-giving change, however, the organization will face certain death, as illustrated by the figure below:

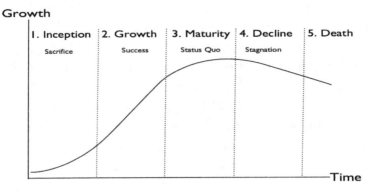

Figure 1: Organizational Lifecycle

Twentieth-century management guru Peter Drucker agrees with the need for disruption:

> Change the organization when you are successful … when everything is going beautifully … when everybody says, "Don't rock the boat. If it ain't [sic] broke don't fix it." … Have the character. Risk being unpopular, and say let's improve.[15]

Meaningful organizational change that brings new life happens when people intentionally disrupt the status quo.

Often in the discussion of promoting the presence of minorities in an organization, those currently in power raise concerns about the dangers of creating quota systems, tokenism, or the appearance of political correctness. However, the issue of cultivating opportunities for minorities does not exist to fulfill a worldly demand nor pacify as an act of compromise; rather, "as a vision of the Kingdom, minority inclusion should remain a priority of the Church."[16] In other words, an inclusive model of leadership is a model demanded by Scripture.

Build Strategic Relationships

Resistance to inclusion occurs against the backdrop of a unique racial narrative in the United States between whites and blacks, which yields a tangible fear among both groups. Whites tend to fear black incompetence, while blacks tend to fear white dominance. Added to this are the difficulties stemming from various narratives of globalism, which reveal the existence of other biases that challenge minority inclusion: "From tribalism, to colorism, to ethnic cleansings, humanity seems to be very attune to quickly observe and respond to difference."[17] Overcoming such challenges requires an intentional approach, such as that proposed by Soong-Chan Rah.

Rah reflects upon the value of strategic relationships through the lens of the shared histories between blacks and whites in America. Rah asserts the existence of a certain "luxury" that benefits those in a cultural majority, while ethnic minorities remain "keenly aware of their status and calibrated toward biases that may be intentionally or unintentionally communicated."[18] Cross-cultural relationships can help bridge these different perspectives by vanquishing false perceptions that can come from living homogeneously, disconnected from people different from oneself.[19]

Avoid Groupthink

One of the unintended consequences of homogeneity in a community or organization results in a phenomenon known as groupthink. Christina Cleveland states that "groupthink occurs when a homogeneous group lacks input, perspective and association from others."[20] Groupthink can negatively impact faith communities in the following ways:

1. They overestimate their invulnerability or high moral stance.

2. They collectively rationalize the decision that they make.

3. They demonize or stereotype other groups and their leaders.

4. They have a culture of uniformity wherein individuals censor themselves and others to maintain a façade of group unanimity.

5. They contain members who take it upon themselves to protect the group leader (usually the pastor) by hoarding, filtering or spinning information.[21]

Groupthink can prove dangerous, especially when missional organizations such as churches begin to reach out cross-culturally with no advocate who can present information and insights of the people group they attempt to reach. Leaders must cultivate diverse teams and foster honest and open communication.

Build Better Relational Dynamics

Scott Williams affirms the need for better relational dynamics between diverse people in the church. He offers four insights for building healthy, multiethnic organizations:

1. Do not embrace the argument of "I do not see color." Our race helps form our understanding of our faith and life, from what we feel about politics, race, culture to how to raise our kids.

2. Although ethnicity is a part of each of our life stories, it doesn't have to confine or limit our thinking.

3. Issues of race are complex, and they are not something that we just sit down and solve. It takes time.

4. There are no dumb questions. ... We must begin to ask the tough questions and begin the necessary discussions to address the issues of church diversity.[22]

Further, churches must remember that nothing can replace the power of grace in relational dynamics. When people pursue life together in community, they engage in a sloppy affair, wrought with misgivings, misunderstandings, and miscommunication. In such an environment, nothing can take the place of redemptive grace. Grace provides the antidote to division and frustration. It serves as the oil that keeps the relationship fluid and free flowing. Grace gives rise to trust; it moves the relationship forward in a way that honors God.[23]

Once people within an organization settle relational insecurities, they can then begin the hard work of building an institution where power does not benefit those at the top but serves all within the organization. Though the antiquated model of twentieth century, top-down hierarchical leadership may be necessary at times, even pragmatic, younger generations require relational connections to their leadership as a basis of determining authenticity and credibility.[24] Increased connectivity builds deeper community, which leads to greater organizational commitment.[25]

Cultivate Racial Inclusion

When minorities enter an unfamiliar space, they often feel compelled to quickly survey the room in an effort to find a person of similar ethnicity, followed by looking for anyone who represents a minority group. The consequences of not finding other minorities in places such as a church results in real consequences, as observed by Gary McIntosh and Daniel Reeves: "No diversity on staff + no diversity on the platform = no diversity in the church."[26] In other words, homogeneity only breeds homogeneity.

> "Breaking a cycle of homogeneity begins with cultivating racial inclusion, so it permeates an organization's culture."

Breaking a cycle of homogeneity begins with cultivating racial inclusion, so it permeates an organization's culture. Transactional means of simply checking boxes to indicate the presence of a handful of diverse individuals remains insufficient.[27] Organizations can create an inclusive culture only by implementing life-giving systems powerful enough to overwrite the current norms and create a new value system.[28] When leaders feel frustrated by cultural norms that lead the organization into drift, they must focus not on changing current culture but by introducing a new, healthy culture.[29] The implementation of team theory may assist in this process.

In his book, *The Teaming Church*, Robert C. Crosby reiterates the purpose of a team to "make the strength of each person effective and his or her personal weakness irrelevant."[30] In applying this to building a culture of inclusion, leaders will view differences as a means of organizational strength. Through the inclusion of diverse voices, the organization will gain something far more than increased production; it will benefit from the souls of individuals, a priceless gain.[31]

Craft a New Vision

The corporate church as a prophetic witness and a redemptive force in society cannot afford the luxury of indifference. It must study its contextual community and cultural landscape and define what successful inclusion looks like—reaching and engaging those within its context.[32] Leaders must craft a vision in light of cultural realities and define their missions accordingly. For the Christian organization, this means utilizing a biblical framework as a reflective tool to provide a value system, one that serves as a foundation to building vision and mission.[33]

Engaging in cross-cultural integration cannot occur amputated from the realities of racism and prejudice, which have fostered "animosity and mistrust."[34] Likewise, the Church cannot overlook as trivial the contemporary realities of biased, unaltered systems that seemingly support past divides. Soong-Chan Rah addresses this point and demonstrates the power of cross-cultural engagement:

> If we do not take the time to reflect on each other's history and story, then we are not ready to engage in cross-cultural ministry. When we hear the stories of others' suffering, we have the opportunity to lament together and then move forward in a positive and authentic manner.[35]

Cross-cultural integration requires listening to each other.

Those in the majority may have concerns engaging cross-culturally; they may even find such engagement as a source of fear. They must understand what happens during such engagements rather than fear them, however. When people enter the stream of conversations concerning race and cross-cultural engagement, they inherit the realities found within, regardless of whether they participated in acts of injustice. For example, sometimes people believe that because they "never owned slaves or have never been a slave" that it "should suffice in moving forward."[36] However, such beliefs prove insufficient for cross-cultural engagement. People must recognize that they have inherited the consequences of history.

> "People must recognize that they have inherited the consequences of history."

An approach that pursues a path forward involves engagement in a manner that gives life, so all can rejoice as they gather around an inclusive table with fresh insights and ideas.[37] This requires acknowledging the inheritance of yesterday's problems and that sin created this current state of affairs. Likewise, it means that these sin problems require spiritual means and realities to address them.[38] The gospel continues to be the good news, and leaders must recognize where God works and discover how they can become involved.[39]

Leaders do not have to solve the problem of cross-cultural engagement; they simply need to seize the opportunity.[40]

Promote a Countercultural Life

Jesus made strong assertions about the functionality of the kingdom of God. He commands followers toward lives built upon seemingly outlandish behaviors, such as loving one's enemies (Luke 6:27), turning the other cheek (Matt 5:39), finding greatness in serving (Mark 10:43), being last in order to become first (Mark 10:31), and losing one's life in order to find it (Matt 10:39). Indeed, this distinctively different life produces a curious prophetic witness, one that heightens the consciousness of the lost, according to Rodney Stark:

> How did a small sect of Judaism become the dominant religion of the Roman Empire within three centuries? … In the example of the treatment of women, … the church chose to hold a respectful view of women and the family that was not the dominant perspective in Roman culture. Likewise, the church's showing compassion to the diseased in the cities revealed a countercultural value system. In both examples, the church sought to uphold biblical values above and beyond the surrounding culture's values. … The church was willing to exhibit and demonstrate these values through the existing cultural context, rather than outside of it. [41]

The Church's moments of shining glory occur when it asserts the clarion message of a countercultural life. Like the Early Church in the Roman Empire, today's Church should remain at the forefront of forming a countercultural response by cultivating multiethnic organizations. This will require, however, prophetic leadership.

Collaborate as a Team

Successfully building an inclusive, multiethnic organization requires collaboration. Through collaborative teamwork, the leader ensures that people at the grass roots level own the vision for the organization.[42] Collaboration gives those at lower levels in the organization an opportunity to embrace, champion, and resource the vision. When people receive the opportunity to build, they typically will; in the end, they will own what they helped build.[43] Healthy, collaborating teams share the following characteristics:

1. The teams are fluid and focused on a task.

2. Team members acquire a deep-seated belief in the power and synergy of teams.

3. Team members experience a climate of trust.

4. Team members practice open and honest communication.

5. Team conflict is viewed as a normal means of exploring new ideas creatively.[44]

Further, a collaborative team must unify around a common goal by "stirring passions" and simply and concretely "creating a common fate."[45]

Collaboration also includes the benefits of mentoring. While collaboration can naturally foster traditional modeling, which remains primarily top-down, manager to subordinate, it can also result in peer-to-peer mentoring, where the sharing of best practices and knowledge moves sideways. Likewise, collaboration increases reverse mentoring,[46] giving rise to a bottom-up flow of information. By utilizing mentoring pathways that naturally tend to exist within collaborative teams, "the currents of information, best practices, and organizational perspectives can be shared in a free-flowing manner."[47] Thus, inclusive and diverse teams will benefit from intentional collaboration.

Understand and Include the Three
Types of Ethnic Leaders

Bryan Loritts describes three types of ethnic leaders.[48] C1 ethnic leaders remain fully immersed in the dominant culture and value cultural acceptance above all. Conversely, C3 ethnic leaders resist cultural assimilation. Their resistance may stem from fears resulting from past history or a desire to protect or preserve ethnic history and uniqueness. C2 ethnic leaders, on the other hand, can fluidly move between their culture and the dominant culture. They possess the ability to preserve their ethnicity while skillfully migrating cross-culturally. Loritts describes C1 leaders as those lacking cultural relevance, C3 leaders as great protestors and voices of injustice, and C2 leaders as bridge builders who can help solve problems that affect ethnic minorities.[49]

Table 5: Three Types of Ethnic Leaders

Type of Leader	Descriptor	Biblical Model	Modern Example
C1- Ethnic & Assimilated	Culturally Absorbed	Hellenist	Carlton Banks from Fresh Prince (fictional)
C3 - Ethnic & Refuse Assimilation	Culturally Inflexible	Pharisees	Al Sharpton
C2 - Ethnic & - Cultural Migration	Culturally Flexible	Paul	Denzel Washington

Loritts stresses that people do not neatly fit within only one type of leadership style, but these three descriptions do offer a tool to understand how people may approach cultural differences. Those operating in the C1 style may have compelling stories of how they overcame adversity, while those leading as a C3 can serve as a voice of conscience, often speaking inconvenient truths to those in power. Finally, a C2 can serve as a great resource, creating compelling narratives for discussion.

Implement New Vision

Begin with Culture

One of the greatest responsibilities a leader has consists of creating organizational vision. However, organizational culture has the capacity to make or a break a vision, regardless of how robust the vision is or how much a leader desires organizational change. Culture has this power because it reflects the accepted norms in a community:[50] "The concept of culture refers to the taken-for-granted values, underlying assumptions, expectations, and definitions that characterize organizations and their members."[51] John Kotter asserts that leading change only happens through changing the organization's culture: "the norms of behavior and shared values among a group of people."[52] The leader's role, then, must focus also on cultivating an organizational culture of inclusion. Leaders must willingly demonstrate the value of inclusion. They must effectively navigate the introduction of a diverse culture with an unyielding commitment, followed by the long-term honing of skills in cross-cultural understanding.[53]

Culture has the power to overwhelm vision, however. As Sam Chand pointedly observes, "Culture eats vision for lunch."[54] He notes that culture possesses the single most dominant factor within an organization, more so than strategy and vision, and likens the development of a new vision or strategy to an organ transplant: "Much like a body will reject a new organ, so culture will attack and negate a new vision."[55] An organization's culture, therefore, requires careful cultivation.

Be Proactive

In pursuing inclusive, multi-ethnic organizations, leaders must remain intentional rather than simply casting a new vision, which "will not cure cultural issues; the only way to change culture is by the introduction of that which is culturally healthy and consistent to facilitate a new vision."[56] Such an intentional approach requires leaders to adopt a proactive approach in practicing inclusion and committing themselves to seeing inclusion manifest. Scott Williams outlines seven practices for remaining intentional as leaders work toward building a culture of inclusion:

1. Check your heart—Start by asking the questions, the right ones, the difficult ones that go to the issues of the heart.

2. Check your head—Face issues of race and ethnicity.

3. Be prayerful—Ask God to give you a burden.

4. Be purposeful.

5. Be prepared for confrontations.

6. Be authentic.

7. Be patient—This is going to take some time.[57]

Patience remains critical. Over time, however, the benefits of an inclusive organization will begin to appear.

The presence of diverse members, for example, will make the organization nimbler in learning. Conversely, when organizations only have leaders with similar experiences, knowledge, and voices, they increase their exposure to blind spots, limited perspectives, and group think. Such a myopic approach provides only limited pools of information, diminishing over time the organization's relevance and ability to be heard by others. Inviting and including diverse perspectives adds to leaders' body of knowledge and creates a wider scope. Further, those who may have felt marginalized will feel included.[58]

As leaders begin to change the culture of the organization by including diverse voices in leadership, they will lay the foundation for casting a new vision for a multi-ethnic organization. Stephen Covey defines vision as the "best manifestation of creative imagination and the primary motivation of human action. It is the ability to see beyond our present reality, to create, to invent what does not yet exist, to become what we not yet are. It gives us capacity to live out our imagination instead of our memory."[59] Casting a new and creative vision requires leaders to "define reality," according to leadership strategist Max DePree.[60] Defining reality means that the leader shoulders the burden and calls for the strength to clearly define current realities and determine a pathway forward toward a preferred future.[61] Effective leaders know how to effectively and clearly define the pathway, such as seen with John F. Kennedy's pronouncement, "We choose to go to the moon," Martin Luther King Jr.'s visionary speech, "I Have a Dream," or Ronald Reagan's defiant command, "Tear down this wall!" Leaders must clearly and effectively communicate the preferred future throughout the organization.

> "As leaders begin to change the culture of the organization by including diverse voices in leadership, they will lay the foundation for casting a new vision for a multi-ethnic organization."

Without such communication, followers merely speculate as to where the organization is headed.[62] Clearly articulated visions remain powerful: "Big dreams are also contagious. They are infectious. They not only change you, but they can also slowly begin to change your friends and those around you! Big dreams generate excitement, and they attract those who want to follow your example and step out in faith."[63] In other words, vision can drive mission.

Vision is powerful not because of its creation but because of what it can cultivate: "Vision can shape values, determine priorities, and define mission."[64] A strong but clear vision has the power to "address a multitude of small decisions. Vision can create new energy and release new life over the organization. It fosters momentum and clarifies the objective. This sort of mission clarity becomes invaluable to the organization."[65] A strong vision, however, requires intentional development, one that considers strategy, objectives, and values.

Carl F. George identifies three pragmatic ways to cast a clear vision:

1. First, you need a game plan—The game plan, then, is your philosophy of ministry. It summarizes your overall strategy and objectives. It needs to be clear enough that you could present it in three or four sentences to your unchurched neighbor who asks, "Exactly what is your church trying to do?"

2. A second factor that helps the vision is the party line— The party line, then, may deal with some very ticklish issues. But it is a necessary ingredient in explaining how a vision will be communicated.

3. A third component of effective vision casting is hero making—The implication for pastors and church leaders is to keep score and then brag on the things they want to see more of. Christians profit from positive role models, whether they come from the hall of champions in Hebrews 11, from a video profile of an amazing volunteer, or from hero-making sermons. As the old adage goes, "Everybody loves a story." [66]

In casting vision, leaders must discern what remains vital to the organization. They must make a long-term vow to the ministry vision but short-term commitments to ministry models. They must reflect passion towards their ministry mission and loosely hold on to their ministry approach.[67]

Navigate Transition with Pastoral Leadership

Leaders who cultivate an inclusive culture and vision know how to successfully navigate the transitions that come from change. They also know the difference between change and transition. Don Brawley III describes the process of change as happening in a moment of time, like getting a new job or giving birth, a moment that is

> tied to the calendar, a singular event that one can document on a personal planner. Transition, on the other hand, refers to the emotional, physical, physiological, financial, sociological, and relational impacts of change. Transition happens over time; it occurs far more slowly than change. Often, when we talk of change management, we really are speaking about managing transition.[68]

Utilizing a biblical lens, leaders of change view change as an apostolic function and transitions as requiring pastoral leadership. Change requires apostolic boldness, courage, and clarity, while navigating transition requires a shepherd-like patience, compassion, and mercy. Leaders can help team members effectively manage change if leaders make them aware of the transitional issues surrounding change. Conversely, if leaders do not take adequate time to address, process, or deal with transitional issues, the team will grow weary.

Leaders navigating transitions will remain cognizant of the three entities needing involvement in the process: God, the leader, and the people. Too often, however, one entity remains left out of the equation, as illustrated below by the zones of change:

Table 6: Leadership Zones of Change

Zone	Description	Relationship
Zone One	Sweet Spot Space	All Together, God + Leader + People
Zone Two	Default Space	God + Leader, without the People
Zone Three	Listening Space	God + People, without the Leader
Zone Four	Danger Space	The Leader + The People, without the Lord

Karl Vaters asserts that successful change can only happen when leaders and people work together with God, putting them in the "sweet spot" of zone one, while frustration and problems will occur in all other zones.[69]

Leaders who desire to see lasting cultural and organizational change as it pertains to building an inclusive, multicultural Acts 2-style church will engage in the following actions with their teams, as outlined by Alton Garrison:

1. Enlist—Cast a clear, compelling vision. Personally interview the person and show the benefits and blessings of serving, not the burden of having to serve.

2. Expect—Explain what is expected of someone serving in a particular role. To quote an old adage: You can't inspect what you haven't expected.

3. Equip—Give a scriptural foundation for the role (biblical examples of service), provide adequate resources, and make sure they function in their gifting and ability.

4. Engage—Actually release them with responsibility and trust them with some level of authority.

5. Evaluate—Review expectations and evaluate performance. This is where accountability comes in.

6. Encourage—Praise them in public; correct them in private.[70]

Implementing long-lasting change requires not only a good idea but intentionality and the "ability to convert ideas into effective results."[71] Leaders cannot simply settle for desiring diversity in leadership for their organizations; they must cultivate the skills and abilities to implement such change.

Conclusion

To recap, then: pastors, Christian leaders, and churches can utilize the following ten principles to facilitate integration and reconciliation:

1. clarify the win
2. exercise your prophetic voice
3. challenge the status quo
   a. find the right time
   b. build strategic relationships
   c. avoid groupthink
   d. build better relational dynamics
4. cultivate racial inclusion
5. craft a new vision
7. promote a countercultural life
8. collaborate as a team
9. understand and include the three types of ethnic leaders
10. implement new vision
    a. begin with culture
    b. be proactive
    c. navigate transition with pastoral leadership

The Assemblies of God as a Pentecostal movement traces its founding back to the Azusa Street Revival. The Azusa outpouring of the Holy Spirit came as a shining star of hope against the dark night of racism and segregation. The leading voice of the Azusa Revival was a black man, William Seymour, who effectively led the nation's first racially inclusive church. Since that beginning, the Assemblies of God has grown organically with congregational demographics that now mirror the United States of the twenty-first century. The Lord has, indeed, fulfilled His promise to pour out His Spirit upon all, regardless of race, ethnicity, gender, age, class, or social standing (Joel 2:28-29).

Despite these advances, however, the absence of minority leaders, especially at the district level, has become the **status quo** for the movement. Cultivating opportunities to identify, train, develop, and deploy new leaders will take a level of courageous leadership, some difficult conversations about racial issues, and the allocation of resources—time, talent, and treasure—to make inclusive leadership a matter of priority. As a sense of urgency builds to bring diverse voices into leadership, the Fellowship can then create a compelling **vision** for inclusive leadership. Crafting a vision for the preferred future often means abandoning old scorecards, taking a long view approach, and redefining success. Crafting this new vision will require **collaboration**, a process in which leaders in the majority invite minority leaders and their voices to the table of leadership. Lastly, it will require relationship building, where the values of trust, transparency, and transformation guide the process.

Building on these ten principles, the following section provides specific action steps AG leaders can take to facilitate black leadership in the movement.

Action Steps for the Assemblies of God

Cultivate Missional Focus and Passionate Affirmation

The Assemblies of God has organically grown to almost mirror the demographic population of the United States. This change has occurred through the work of the Holy Spirit. The cultivation mandate explored in my doctoral project's biblical-theological review compels the Fellowship to organize and bring systems and processes necessary to ensure that the fruit of the Spirit yields "fruit that remains" (John 15:16). Producing fruit that remains informs the deeply rooted missiology of the Assemblies of God: "Dedicated to [Christ] for the greatest evangelism that the world has ever seen."[72] The changing demographic of the United States and this Fellowship requires missional focus and passionate affirmation of minority leaders.

Address the Lingering Problem of Perception

This book also points to a lingering perception problem within the Assemblies of God. When black leaders share that they belong to the Assemblies of God, their peers quizzically ask why. Many still hold the perception that the Fellowship remains a primarily white denomination, just as it had for several decades in the twentieth century. Many do not realize that in recent decades the denomination has grown and continues to grow significantly diverse. The Fellowship has done well in utilizing inclusive photos and print materials, as well as featuring news stories on leaders of color, which can assist in aligning perceptions about demographics with reality.

Acknowledge the Growing
Complexity of Labels

One of the challenges I encountered while implementing my doctoral project concerned how people use the term *African American*. As the Assemblies of God has grown, especially among its African and Caribbean constituencies, the term no longer serves as an all-inclusive racial descriptor for black people in the Fellowship. Further, a generational dynamic complicates the use of the term. Millennials perceive the use of African American as disingenuous because they feel no connection to Africa. The simple racial descriptors of the past prove insufficient in today's racially and ethnically complex society.

See and Connect with the Only
Black Person in the Room

The term *minority* means that, numerically, a majority exists. This often means that when a leader of color enters the room, the leader may find no one else who shares the same ethnic background, gender, culture, or skin color. Such situations create feelings of isolation, requiring the minority leader to muster strength and ego to navigate the room and suppress feelings of doubt and uncertainty. For minority leaders, such situations physically exhaust them. Majority leaders, then, have a responsibility to make leaders of color feel valued and celebrated. Affirmation does not happen through trite compliments, however. It requires true connections, listening to stories, and seeing others as valued individuals.

Develop Minority Leadership Opportunities at the National Level

To cultivate leadership opportunities for minorities, the Fellowship's national leaders should grant each district an additional general presbyter (GP) and designate the positions for ethnic minorities. The national leadership has already set this precedent by establishing general presbyter positions for women and those under forty years of age, as well as with the designation at the executive presbytery level of seats for a black executive presbyter, a woman, and a person under forty years of age. I also concur with a recommendation by Dr. Shannon Polk in her Doctor of Ministry project, "Creating Pathways to Leadership for Women of Color in the Assemblies of God," when she says, "An official study from the [Assemblies of God] would elicit more participation than a doctoral student project can produce."[73] Such a study would entail a qualitative analysis of minority leaders.[74]

Develop Inclusive and Diverse Districts

Valuing inclusion and promoting a culture of diversity remain paramount for cultivating leadership opportunities for minorities. Districts should extend invitations to key leaders of color to collaborate on relationship building and leadership pipeline development. Promoting this culture, however, requires a long-term commitment by districts rather than simply accomplishing a few actionable items. Districts should also explore ethnic fellowships and consider establishing district chapters of the Black Fellowship. Districts can also use the power of appointment to create opportunities for minority leaders to serve on committees, within sections, and on district executive presbyteries. District leaders could also allow minority credential holders to caucus and self-select leaders.

Districts should also intentionally invite speakers of color to events such as minister retreats, district councils, and schools of ministry. They should also find ways to mentor leaders of color. By investing in minority leaders, districts can build awareness and benefit from a shared future. In return, district leaders will benefit from reverse mentoring as minority leaders share their insights and expertise. In addition, districts may need to provide financial assistance to minority leaders from smaller and poorer churches, so they may attend district events.

Finally, in finding minority speakers, districts should utilize the National Black Fellowship (https://nbfag.org/), which provides a pool of black credential holders with myriad strengths, areas of expertise, and ministry contexts. Districts can also partner with the NBF to create a strategic plan of engagement for minority communities. The NBF offers excellent resources for fostering relationships with black leaders in the Assemblies of God.

Promote Self-Development among Black Leaders

Black leaders need to engage their districts and attend district sponsored events. They need to tap into the hearts and visions of district leaders and partner on projects and other endeavors. Black leaders must reflect value their distinctiveness and ministry contexts, while also living out the ethos of the Assemblies of God. Finally, as the Christian motivational speaker, Jim Rohn, says, "Work harder on yourself than you work at your job."[75] In other words, black leaders must engage in self-development and self-improvement. This prepares them to lead when opportunities present themselves.

---

[1] Scott Williams, *Church Diversity: Sunday the Most Segregated Day of the Week* (Green Forest, AR: New Leaf Press, 2011), 78, Kindle.
[2] Mark DeYmaz and Harry Li, *Leading a Healthy Multi-Ethnic Church: Seven Common Challenges and How to Overcome Them*, The Leadership Network Innovation Series

(Grand Rapids, MI: Zondervan, 2010), 36, Kindle.

3 Williams, *Church Diversity*, 94.

4 Reggie Joiner, Lane Jones, and Andy Stanley, *Seven Practices of Effective Ministry* (Sisters, OR: Multnomah Publishers, 2004), 71.

5 Ibid., 78.

6 Everett M. Rogers, *Diffusion of Innovations* (New York: Free Press, 1995), 23.

7 DeYmaz and Li, *Leading a Healthy Multi-Ethnic Church*, 25.

8 Ibid.

9 Gilbreath, *Reconciliation Blues*, 134, Kindle.

10 Ibid., 952-953, Kindle.

11 Williams, *Church Diversity*, 150.

12 Samuel R. Chand, *Cracking Your Church's Culture Code: Seven Keys to Unleashing Vision and Inspiration* (San Francisco: Josey-Bass, 2011), 176, Apple Books.

13 Ibid., 179.

14 Ibid.

15 Peter F. Drucker, *Managing the Non-Profit Organization: Practices and Principles* (New York: Routledge, 1990), 66.

16 DeYmaz and Li, *Leading a Healthy Multi-Ethnic Church*, 38.

17 Burton Andrew Ross, interview by Darnell K. Williams, Sr, Florence, SC, October 5, 2018.

18 Rah, *Many Colors*.

19 Cleveland, *Disunity in Christ*, 171.

20 Ibid.

21 Ibid., 41-42.

22 Williams, *Church Diversity*, 138.

23 David A. Anderson, *Gracism: The Art of Inclusion* (Wheaton, IL: IVP, 2007), 887, Kindle.

24 Leroy Barber, *Red, Brown, Yellow, Black, White: Who's More Precious in God's Sight?* (New York: Jericho Books, 2014), 362, Kindle.

25 Joseph R. Myers, *The Search to Belong: Rethinking Intimacy, Community, and Small Groups* (Grand Rapids, MI: Zondervan, 2003), 309, Kindle.

26 Williams, *Church Diversity*, 61.

27 Frederick A. Miller and Judith H. Katz, *Inclusion Breakthrough: Unleashing the Real Power of Diversity* (Oakland, CA: Berrett-Koehler Publishers, 2002), 236, Kindle.

28 Ibid., 500, Kindle.

29 Gary McIntosh and R. Daniel Reeves, *Thriving Churches in the Twenty-First Century: 10 Life-Giving Systems for Vibrant Ministry* (Grand Rapids, MI: Kregel Publications, 2006), 37.

30 Robert C. Crosby, *The Teaming Church: Ministry in the Age of Collaboration* (Nashville, TN: The United Methodist Publishing House, 2012), 25.

31 Miller and Katz, *Inclusion Breakthrough*, 367, Kindle.

32 McIntosh and Reeves, *Thriving Churches*, 27.

33 Ibid., 29.

34 Rah, *Many Colors*, 56.

35 Ibid., 59.

36 Anderson, *Gracism*, 115.

37 Ibid., 119.

38 Mark DeYmaz, *Re:Mix: Transitioning Your Church to Living Color* (Nashville: Abingdon Press, 2016), 289, Kindle.

39 DeYmaz, *Re:Mix*, 289, Kindle.

40 Miller and Katz, *Inclusion Breakthrough*, 312, Kindle.

41 Rodney Stark, *The Rise of Christianity: How the Obscure, Marginal Jesus Movement Became the Dominate Religious Force in the Western World in a Few Centuries* (Princeton, NJ: Princeton University Press, 1996), 3.

42 McIntosh and Reeves, *Thriving Churches*, 111.

43 Rich Guerra, superintendent of Southern California Network of the Assemblies of God, interview with Darnell Williams, Lima, OH, February 14, 2019.

44 McIntosh and Reeves, *Thriving Churches*, 113.

45 Morten T. Hansen, *Collaboration: How Leaders Avoid the Traps, Create Unity, and Reap Big Results* (Boston: Harvard Business Press, 2009), 77-81.

46 Earl Creps, *Reverse Mentoring: How Young Leaders Can Transform the Church and Why We Should Let Them* (Hoboken, NJ: Wiley Publishing, 2008).

47 McIntosh and Reeves, *Thriving Churches*, 93.

48 Bryan Loritts, *Right Color, Wrong Culture: A Leadership Fable* (Chicago: Moody, 2014), 122.

49 Ibid.

50 Kim Cameron and Robert Quinn, *Diagnosing and Changing Organizational Culture: Based on the Competing Values Framework* (San Francisco: Jossey-Bass, 2006), 83.

51 Troy Jones, *Recalibrate Your Church: How Your Church Can Reach Its Full Kingdom Impact* (Amazon Digital Services: Recalibrate Group, 2016), 69, Kindle.

52 John Kotter, *Leading Change* (Boston: Harvard Business Review, 2012), 157.

53 David Livermore, *Cultural Intelligence: Improving Your CQ to Engage Our Multicultural World* (Grand Rapids, MI: Baker Academic), 14.

54 Samuel Chand, *Cracking Your Church's Culture Code*, 21.

55 Ibid.

56 Andy Crouch, *Culture Making: Recovering Our Creative Calling* (Downers Grove, IL: InterVarsity Press, 2008), 64, 66.

57 Williams, *Church Diversity*, 45-47.

58 Cleveland, *Disunity in Christ*, 184.

59 Alton Garrison, *A Spirit-Empowered Church: An Acts 2 Ministry Model* (Springfield, MO: Influence Resources, 2015), 1240-1243, Kindle.

60 Mark D. Roberts, "God as the Leader Who Defines Reality," Life for Leaders, April 18, 2015, https://lifeforleaders.depree.org/god-as-the-leader-who-defines-reality/, quoted in Karl Vaters, *Small Church Essentials: Field-Tested Principles for Leading a Healthy Congregation of Under 250* (Chicago: Moody, 2018), 1112-1114, Kindle.

61 Carl F. George and Warren Bird, *How to Break Growth Barriers: Revise Your Role, Release Your People, and Capture Overlooked Opportunities for Your Church* (Grand Rapids, MI: Baker, 2017), 35, Kindle.

62 Ibid.

63 Jones, *Recalibrate Your Church*, 189.

64 Garrison, *A Spirit-Empowered Church*, 1264-1265, Kindle.

65 Jones, *Recalibrate Your Church*, 189.

66 George, *How to Break Growth Barriers*, 56.

67 Jones, *Recalibrate Your Church*, 108.

68 Don Brawley III, interview with the author, Columbus, Ohio, June 25, 2015.

69 Vaters, *Small Church Essentials*, 1687-1690, Kindle.

70 Garrison *A Spirit-Empowered Church*, 2177, 2181, 2185, Kindle.

71 Drucker, *Managing the Non-profit*, 66.

72 World AG Fellowship, "History of WAGF," World AG Fellowship, accessed

November 1, 2019, https://worldagfellowship.org/Fellowship/History-of-WAGF.

73 Shannon Polk, "Creating Pathways to Leadership for Women of Color in the Assemblies of God," (DMin project, Assemblies of God Theological Seminary, 2017), http://agts.edu/wp-content/uploads/2017/07/24q_Polk.pdf, 146.

74 Ibid.

75 Jim Rohn, "Work Harder on Yourself, Not on Your Job" (video), YouTube, August 15, 2016, accessed November 1, 2019, https://youtu.be/1zNx3QyQ-9M.

7 Appreciative Inquiry as a Tool for Navigating Change and Cultivating Leadership Opportunities

Why Appreciative Inquiry?

This field project associated with my doctoral project revealed that AG leaders have two basic approaches toward cultivating leadership opportunities for African-Americans: (1) a proactive approach that fosters creativity and asks how the organization can serve the vision, a pragmatic "get it done" approach. This approach provides a safe, grace-filled space that fosters intimacy and relational growth. (2) The other approach reflects a scarcity mindset as it pertains to resources, personnel, and candidates. In this approach, past failures breed hesitancy in investing in diverse leadership, feelings reinforced by organizational rationales as to why such initiatives do not work. The lack of external strategic partners being invited to the table and being allowed to dream together and determine a preferred future created an absence of creativity and innovation.

Utilizing Appreciative Inquiry (AI) as the change model was an intentional decision. As a tool, AI demands a focus that begins with the positive and builds from that point forward. It requires one to acknowledge the best of what is. The Assemblies of God has a long history of attempting to grapple with the question of blacks and leadership. Dating back to 1915 when it ordained its first black minister, Ellsworth S. Thomas of Binghamton, NY; to the 1950s story of Bob Harrison and the question of the creation of a "Colored Branch" of the AG (an idea that was abandoned); to the 1980s and the formation of the Inner-City Workers Conference and its evolution into the National Black Fellowship of the Assemblies of God. Loads of good work has already been done, which does not diminish the better and best works that still need to be pursued.

The Appreciative Inquiry Process

What is Appreciative Inquiry?

Appreciative Inquiry (AI) is an asset based, positive change process model. It celebrates current momentum, while looking to the future. AI implements intentional steps that ensure a new goal is achieved.

How does the process flow?

1. Discovery – The Best of What is – Appreciation
2. Dream – Imagine What Could Be – Possibility
3. Design – Determine What Should Be – Construction
4. Destiny – Create What Will Be – Innovation

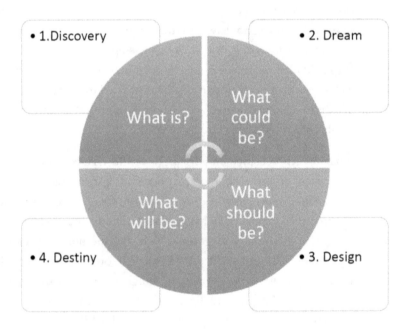

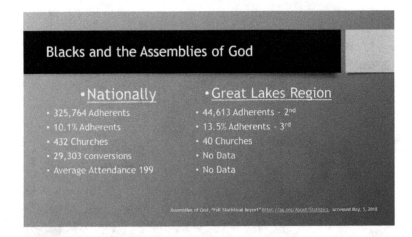

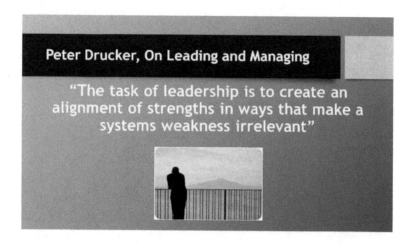

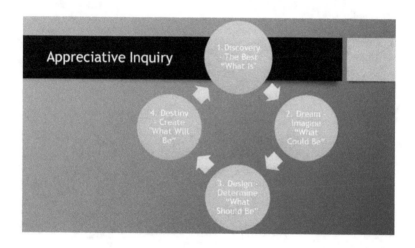

Discovery - The Best "What Is"

•Think Appreciation...

1. Discovery - The Best "What Is"

- 1979 - Birth of AG ICWC/AG National Black Fellowship
- 1994 - The Memphis Miracle
- 1997 - Resolution 22 - Creation of Commission on Ethnicity
- 2007 - Election of First Black ELT Member - Dr. Zollie Smith
- 2014 - Multi-Ethnic Task Force Report - Value Ethnic Diversity
- 2015 - Election of First Black EP - Dr. Sam Huddleston
- 2017- Election Of Malcolm Burleigh - US Missions

1. Discovery - The Best "What Is"

Biblical Models - The Old Testament - Adam and Eve
· Cultivation - Missio Dei through Imago Dei
· Orthodoxy and Orthopraxy

When the first parents received the mandate from the Lord to exercise rulership over the earth, they also received spiritual authority from God.

· The Hebrew word for *cultivate* (*`abad*) means "to work or serve," which conveys the necessity of human engagement and involvement.

1. Discovery - The Best "What Is"

Biblical Models - The Old Testament - Joseph
· Pharaoh did not hesitate to appoint Joseph, despite him being a Hebrew, a slave, and a prisoner in Egypt. Joseph was equipped for the task, and Egypt's king cultivated the space for him to lead. The model Pharaoh sets forth goes far beyond mere toleration, too. Joseph receives real power to make significant decisions and influence lasting change, which indicates that Pharaoh deeply appreciated what Joseph could bring leadership:

· "Appreciation is not toleration. When you tolerate someone (meaning you put up with or endure them), you dismiss that person as having little value to you or as someone who doesn't make a significant contribution. To appreciate a person (meaning you recognize his quality, significance, or magnitude, or admire him greatly), you must make an intentional effort to see the very best in that individual. In this context, appreciating someone is not saying thank you, though that is important. It is seeing the value, worth, and quality in that individual."

1. Discovery - The Best "What Is"

Biblical Models - The Old Testament - Ruth

The Book of Ruth demonstrates how the minority stranger needed the care and compassion of one who is well established. It demonstrates how Ruth was the benefactor of the care of Naomi and the compassion of Boaz. Often those in the minority need a heroes and champions. This individuals who are willing to create the space for them. Such relationships typically don't just develop organically. The demand that the insider embrace the stranger and assist them in finding success. The relationships must be intentional, build upon trust, with the insider willing to leverage their power and influence on the behalf of the outsider. Such relationships cannot be built by utilization of often short sighted, transactional means. These relationship must fostered, and nurtured over time.

1. Discovery - The Best "What Is"

Biblical Models - The Old Testament - Daniel

• Daniel serves the rulers of Babylon with a mark of distinction. During his lifetime, the kingdom experiences a change of leadership three times: from Nebuchadnezzar to his son Belshazzar, to Darius the Mede, and finally, Cyrus the Persian. The Scriptures note that Nebuchadnezzar falls on his face to pay homage to Daniel and commands others to make an offering to Daniel (Dan 2:26). Belshazzar honored Daniel, making him third in line to the throne (5:29). Daniel also prospered under the rules of Darius and Cyrus (6:28). Valued by these leaders for his gifting and leadership abilities, Daniel never compromises his Hebrew identity. Instead, Daniel builds respect, rapport, and relationship with others.

1. Discovery - The Best "What Is"

Biblical Models - The Old Testament - Tribal Representation

The most natural action for an inexperienced leader is to construct teams that are reflective of people with similar gifting and perspectives. Void of intentionality, leaders can find themselves constructing teams that lack diversity. The leadership of Moses provides a proactive approach to ensure inclusivity is reflected at the team level. By selecting Tribal Representatives, Moses allows for the cultivation of leaders, tribe by tribe.

1. Discovery - The Best "What Is"

• New Testament - Luke & the Gospel of the Marginalized

The gospel of Luke declares for us that often leaders can appear from those in the margins and minorities. From his declaration that birth of Christ was witnessed by both angels and lowly shepherds (2:15); to the ministry of John the Baptist (3:3-20); to the call of the Apostles, most having been fisherman (Luke 6:13); to the band of women who followed and funded the ministry of Christ (Luke 8:1-3). Luke makes a compelling argument for the cultivation of leaders who are on the fringes. Often they only need a strong leader, willing call them forth and take a risk on them succeeding.

1. Discovery - The Best "What Is"

The New Testament - Representative Leadership in the Diaconate

Often seemingly well-meaning statements such as the affirmation being color blind, can ring hollow with those in a cultural minority. Such as statement can cause a minority to feel that they must suppress cultural differences or avoid voicing input and insights that differ from their counterparts. This can cause unintended consequences of creating blind-spots, hindering the benefits of the minority perspective and ultimately creating an organization that is challenged in learning, modifying or growing.

1. Discovery - The Best "What Is"

The New Testament - The Antioch Church

The visitation of the grace of God to the Greeks of Antioch creates a new identity in the Church. The Greek Christians bypass Judaism with a different and new route to God, one entirely dependent on Christ but without any compliance with the Law of Moses. In response, the Jewish establishment questions the validity of the Greeks' conversion experiences. They questioned how the Greeks could be truly connected to Christ and to their patriarch Abraham without keeping the Law. They did not understand how these *ethnos* could find acceptance and benefit from God's favor apart from adherence to the Law. The conversion of the believers at Antioch sent shock waves to Jerusalem.

1. Discovery - The Best "What Is"

The New Testament - The Jerusalem Council

Not surprisingly, given the Apostle Peter's biases and struggles with the acceptance of Gentiles, the Council chose him to speak first (Acts 10, 11; 15:5-11). The Holy Spirit uses Peter's encounter with Cornelius to validate the idea that salvation remains available to Gentiles. The text implies that if Peter offers the first endorsement of Gentile salvation, then their salvation must truly be an authentic movement from Christ.

1. Discovery - The Best "What Is"

The New Testament - Empowered Females Leaders Thriving in a Patriarchal Culture

• Marvin Richardson Vincent describes Luke's writings as "the Gospel of Womanhood." His portrayal of women in his writings stands in contrast to the world of the New Testament, in which society typically did not hold women in high regard. Women's status ranked alongside those of children, the poor, and other marginalized individuals. Women lived lives of subjection and strictly defined roles with clear responsibilities. Luke's writing provides a platform for recognizing the worthiness of women. His platform creates a thread of honor for women who lead in the Early Church.

1. Discovery - The Best "What Is"

The New Testament - Every Tribe Vision of John

Race is a unique conversation in the American Church. An inclusive approach to church leadership cannot be implemented by over-simplified means nor through the absence of honest conversation. Thankfully, the United States Assemblies of God has been blessed to experience congregational inclusiveness and diversity that allows for celebration, the singing of a new song as it were, yet the absence of this same diversity in leadership should result in prophetic lament and determination to shift toward a vision of the Kingdom.

2. Dream - Imagine "What Could Be"

• Think Possibility....

2. Dream - Imagine "What Could Be"

1. **How to proactively address racial reconciliation in the US Church?**
   - Segregated Sundays - Politics a New Driving Force
   - Yelling and Screaming vs. Speaking and Listening Culture
   - The Forgotten Black Journey & AG Credential Holders
   - Us vs. Them - The Problem of Both Camps Racially
   - Relationship Building across racial lines

2. Dream - Imagine "What Could Be"

2. Politics, Religion & The Conversation
- The Obama Era - First Black and most Politically Liberal President
- The Trump Era - Moral Alignment with Evangelicals, yet lack of Morality
- Re-living Past Pains
- People prefer to worship with those who are aligned politically
- Politics From the Pulpit - Address Issues
- Trouble for Diverse Conversation

2. Dream - Imagine "What Could Be"

3. The Need to Build Bridges
- Mutual Respect
- Need for Conversation
- Understanding, Gaps in Knowledge

- **4. ACMR**
  - Problem with Self Identification
  - Non-Scientific Process
  - Unique Communities - Diversity in Churches

8 Appreciative Inquiry Results

Workshop in Detroit, Michigan

The first appreciative inquiry workshop associated with my doctoral project occurred in Detroit, Michigan, on Tuesday, August 28, 2018, from 1:00 p.m. to 2:30 p.m. as part of the cohort's annual retreat. We met in the café located in Freedom Christian Assembly. Due to one absent cohort member and another one who arrived toward the end of the presentation, six of the eight cohort members fully attended the workshop. I began the workshop by opening the session with prayer. I then gave my PowerPoint presentation and distributed hard copies of the slides and articles. I explained to them why the Fellowship needs more opportunities for diverse leadership, especially for black leaders. I then provided statistics on black adherents in the Assemblies of God, noting the contrast in statistics between the national Fellowship and the Great Lakes Fellowship. I pointed out how black adherents comprise nearly 14 percent of Great Lakes region in comparison to only 10 percent nationally.[1]

Table 7: Blacks in the Assemblies of God

	Nationally	*Great Lakes*
Total Adherents	325,764	44,613
Black Adherents	10.1%	13.5%
Black Churches	432	40
Conversions	29,303	No Data
Average Attendance	199	No Data

I then discussed the process of appreciative inquiry, explaining that it provides a four-step, asset-based approach to problem solving:

- Step 1: Discovery – Recognize the Best of What Is (Celebration)

- Step 2: Dream – Imagine What Could Be (Possibility)
- Step 3: Design – Determine What Should Be (Construction)
- Step 4: Destiny – Create What Will Be (Innovation)

For this first workshop, our discussion focused primarily on steps one and two, and we celebrated the following achievements within the Fellowship: the birth of Assemblies of God Inner Cities Workers Conference, which evolved to become the AG National Black Fellowship (1979), Memphis Miracle (1994), Resolution 22 and the creation of the Commission on Ethnicity (1997); election of Zollie Smith, the first black member of the executive leadership (2007); the Multi-Ethnic Task Force Report and ethnic diversity value (2014); and the election of the first black executive presbyter, Sam Huddleston (2015). As we dialogued about step one, participants then began doing step two, imagining what could be.

Results of the Project Part 1: First Appreciative Inquiry Workshop

After presenting the positive strides toward diverse and inclusive leadership within the Assemblies of God, participants engaged in step two of the AI process by dialoguing about what the Fellowship and the broader Church can do to create even more opportunities. They began speaking about possibilities while also acknowledging lingering frustration and barriers. Participants made five observations during this process.

Observation 1: The Need to Address Racial Reconciliation in the Church

The group noted how strongly Sundays remain segregated and how politics predominately fall along racial lines. They agreed that divisions have grown deeper, as illustrated by the interpersonal interactions on social media. One participant noted that the typical AG credential holder is male, white, and around sixty years old, indicating disconnect from the black journey in America. Participants expressed concern for overcoming the "us vs. them" default position and how to "build bridges that value all our brothers and sisters."

Observation 2: Politics, Religion and the Conversation

One participant said he could not understand how a black Christian can vote for Democrats. I explained the conflict among some black Christians like myself, noting that as both a black man and a godly man, I felt conflicted by President Obama. I felt pride as the first black man ascended to the land's highest office, a stark contrast to our slave past, Jim Crow history, and institutionalized racism, but I also felt frustrated by his liberal platform. We then discussed the conflicts long faced by blacks in the U.S., remembering how enslaved blacks embraced the truth of the master's religion while also rejecting the notion that they lacked true personhood.

Participants then shared their conflict over Donald Trump, who lacks morality and humility yet exists as a standard bearer of conservativism. In response, I chided, "Welcome to my world!" A participant also noted how people now prefer to worship with those who vote like them, which threatens white-led, multiethnic churches, where pastors remain more likely to address issues for white Republicans than issues impacting Democratic black and brown members. The group agreed that the Church prioritizes politics and race over our identities as citizens of the kingdom of God. The group also agreed that only honest conversations can help close gaps in understanding each other.

Observation 3: The Problem
with the ACMR

One participant noted that the Annual Church Ministries Report (ACMR) may provide skewed data due to three issues: as self-identifying reporting, it may reflect perspectives rather than facts. Second, the local churches cannot ensure its accuracy because they lack necessary systems. Third, diverse churches may inaccurately report their data on the ACMR because of how they perceive themselves or wish to be perceived. In other words, in this participant's view, the ACMR may reflect more subjective aspirational hopes rather than "hard facts."

Observation 4: Confronting Scarcity

Much discussion ensued around the scarcity of black leaders. Participants mentioned the absence of a pipeline to develop and prepare black leaders. Someone asked, "Where do we turn to find them? Where is the pool? The National Black Fellowship? The Ethnic Fellowships?" Another noted, "If I had leaders of color, I would do more, but they are absent." One participant cautioned that they should not over-complicate this process. He noted that, just like with anyone else, leaders need to find young, emerging leaders and plug them into district schools of ministry or Assemblies of God schools. One participant emphatically pleaded, "Please let us stop poaching from the Church of God in Christ! We need to create our own pool of leaders!"

I shared a little-known phenomenon about staff members of color at large churches not being encouraged by the district or national Fellowship to seek credentials. As district leaders, they resolved to engage these staff members; however, they also noted that, given our governance model, this may prove difficult. Some noted this problem not only affects leaders of color but also younger leaders.

Younger leaders view ordination more as a financial tax than a greater opportunity to lead and serve.

Observation 5: Ethnic Churches and the AG Ethos

The conversation then discussed the realities of first-generation minority and ethnic churches. The group noted that first generation ethnic churches preserve the language and traditions of their homeland as they seek to connect to their ethnic past. However, the second generation tends to abandon the traditions and language, opting to become more American in lifestyle. The group expressed that ethnic churches need to embrace the Assemblies of God ethos, particularly in the areas of world missions support and raising up missionaries. Some observed that engaging in kid's camp, BGMC, and youth fine arts raises the AG ethos in these churches. Another noted that missions giving within ethnic churches seems low, which raised a question over whether missions giving reflects a spiritual or cultural activity.

I reminded the group that most black Assemblies of God churches are first-generation churches with charter members and the founder as lead pastor. These congregations remain apostolic in their perspective, carving a pathway for the future. They have not benefited from plots of land purchased by a former generation, nor do they have a mortgage-free facility or even a full-time pastor. One participant commented in response, "Honestly, I am frustrated as a district superintendent. I have made the greatest investment in black leaders, and this is where I get the least return on investment." His comments focused on the issues of funding inner city ministries as well as assisting investing in facilities.

Concluding the discussion, participants asked me how I describe a successful outcome for this project. I shared four goals: (1) increased identification, promotion, and development of high capacity, black leaders; (2) created space for those leaders to be seen and heard; (3) a shift from organic growth of minority leaders to intentional cultivation; and (4) the creation of leadership opportunities for black leaders at the sectional, district, and national levels.

---

[1] Assemblies of God, "Full Statistical Report," General Council of the Assemblies of God, accessed May 5, 2018, https://ag.org/About/Statistics.

9 Results of Interviews with Innovative Leaders, Second Workshop, and Black Credential Holders Survey

Introduction

Approximately six months after the first workshop, I conducted five interviews with innovative leaders cultivating diversity in leadership, which yielded valuable insights I would later use during the second appreciative inquiry workshop with the Great Lakes Regional Superintendent Cohort. Four of the interviews occurred during the Joint World Missions-U.S. Missions Retreat held February 11 to 14, 2019, in Puerto Vallarta, Mexico. I conducted the fifth interview via telephone, on February 6, 2019, with Duane Durst, superintendent of the New York Ministry Network.

The following August, I sent out the Black Credential Holders Survey via email. Of the 154 emails I sent, seventy bounced back with invalid email addresses. The leaders of the NBF also forwarded the survey link to individuals in their sphere of influence. In total, forty-six individuals completed the survey.

During this same month, I traveled to Kingston, Tennessee to conduct the second AI workshop at the cohort's annual retreat. Five of the seven original participants attended. I presented a PowerPoint with an overview of appreciative inquiry (AI) and review of our first meeting, along with the findings of my biblical literature and contemporary literature reviews.[1] We then discussed steps three and four of the AI process as it pertains to cultivating black leaders in the Assemblies of God. I also gave each participant a hardcopy of the presentation.

Results of Second Appreciative Inquiry Workshop

At the second appreciate inquiry workshop I conducted during the annual retreat of the Great Lakes Regional Superintendents Cohort, on August 28, 2019, the five participants discussed steps three and four of the AI process as it pertains to cultivating black leaders in the Assemblies of God. As we dialogued, participants identified four issues present in cultivating leadership opportunities for black leaders. The first concerns fairness, equity, and purpose. One participant frankly observed that the AG's lack of "representation by minority leaders did not happen by accident. It happened by intentional choices in our history; the only way to correct these past errors is now by pursuing with purpose."

Often there exists a generational difference over the issue of tokenism. Older boomer blacks have lived through a period where organizations would be guilty of promoting individuals to meet a required quota. For those with this paradigm, the thought of intentionality, like creating a "black" position can be reminiscent of a quota system past. As Generation X are now approaching middle aged living, they may interpret this intentionality as a righting of past wrongs. Further, Millennials may resound with their Boomer elders yet by using a social justice lens, they adopt the posture of their Gen-X predecessors.

The second issue concerned having qualified representation without resorting to tokenism. Participants did not want tokenism, with one saying, "There is no end to that parade." The group agreed that opportunities created for the underrepresented needs competent individuals to fill them. This issue then led to the group identifying a third issue, the need for a leadership pipeline. One participant spoke about developing a cultivating initiative that focuses on identifying minority leaders. The leader stressed that the initiative needs to quickly become more collaborative. Finally, the group identified relationship building as having the power to create opportunities. As one participant noted, "It all comes down to relationships. We can have all the right process and good intentions, but if we are not willing to build relationships [across cultures and with minorities], then none of this will work." We concluded the discussion with need to have hero leaders, those who willingly open the doors of opportunity to champion this issue.

Results of Interviews with Innovative Leaders

Rich Guerra

Rich Guerra, superintendent of the Southern California Network, is the first Latino elected to lead a non-Spanish language district, which also includes the largest Spanish district in the Assemblies of God.[2] Guerra boldly stated his goal to build the most ethnically diverse AG district in the United States. He shared his heart concerning the need for minority leaders: the ethnically diverse, those under forty, and women. He noted that "our minority leaders are unelectable," explaining that "if you are unknown, you are virtually unelectable. However, as people begin to see your ability, your talents, your giftings and capacity, then they have a level of confidence in your competence." He cautioned that the need centers not on entitlement but rather opportunity.

Guerra celebrates that "40 percent of the Executive Presbytery is now comprised of ethnic minorities," and he strives to accommodate minorities rather than assimilate them: "Assimilation is a denying of one's self to be accepted into the majority; accommodation is when the leader creatively makes space for the minority."

The leader must see the value of inclusion and willingly create space for minorities in decision making. He also affirmed the need for "true leaders rather than tokens." He defined token leaders as those "moved into position without access to power and authority. They cannot make decisions or let their voice be heard." Often, he observed ethnic leaders will "over-compensate" to gain respect and to legitimize their presence in the room. He expressed that minority leaders must shift from hiddenness to exposure, but he acknowledged that will only happen if their leaders create opportunities for them.

Guerra outlined four ways that AG leaders can help break the status quo: first, they must rekindle the apostolic, pioneering spirit by being "bold about promoting ethnic leadership like our forefathers were bold in advancing the movement." Second, he encourages ethnic and minority leaders to remain courageous because "currently, I don't have one resumé from a minority or a woman seeking ministry opportunity on my desk." Third, he recommends building unique partnerships such as the one he forged with the Church of God in Christ to train leaders and plant churches. Finally, he believes that each district should model themselves after the General Council in promoting minority and ethnic leaders, those under forty, women, and black general presbyters and executive presbyters. He concluded that if districts did this, "it wouldn't take much effort for us to win at this issue."

Sam Huddleston

Dr. Sam Huddleston serves as the assistant superintendent of the Northern California and Nevada District of the Assemblies of God and is the first elected black executive presbyter.[3] Huddleston described the Fellowship's current governance model by election as perpetuating the status quo. He said that Assemblies of God leaders must utilize the power of appointment to give opportunities to minorities and ethnic leaders. In countering arguments that appointments contribute to quotas or tokenism, he cited the issue of nepotism: "We need to use whatever we need to use to give people opportunity. … We cannot fear quotas while also declaring nepotism as okay. If we can't use the tools of appointment and intentionality, please tell what tools we will use."

He also described the sort of tongue-in-cheek inquiries from some leaders requesting "more leaders like you, Sam." He explained that they want "readymade, polished people. They don't know that the first [white] pastor that hired me had to accept me in the rough state in which he found me—often angry and frustrated." He encourages people of color to prepare themselves so when opportunity comes, they are "promotable. … As an elected officer, you are not an employee; it is a game changer understanding that you are around the table as a peer and equal."

Huddleston then shared his strong conviction that if "we want inclusion, we must reflect it in staffing and even in publications. Our advertisements and the speakers at our gatherings must reflect who we are. They must look like us." He gave an example that if a leadership conference has all male white speakers, then it communicates an unintentional message to women and minorities—they are not welcome.

Finally, he shared with sadness how politics have impacted the Church, noting the negative experience of his nephew at an AG school when President Obama got elected. His professor said, "Let's pray for our nation because right now we don't have a President." Huddleston concluded, "The Pauline instruction to pray for those in authority is not party based and should not shift around if you personally like the person or not."

Brent Allen and Sam Huddleston

Brent Allen, superintendent of the Northern California and Nevada District of the Assemblies of God, joined Sam Huddleston to discuss multiethnic churches and leadership.[4] Allen began the conversation by sharing his experiences in pastoring and leading a multiethnic congregation. In the context of ethnic congregants, he noted that while the church's core mission "is to impact the world, it takes a different skillset to pastor when the world impacts your church." He also asserted that, given the governance model of the AG, in order for ethnic and minorities to occupy positions of leadership, they must receive opportunities to demonstrate their gifts: "They need positive exposure."

Allen's experience leading a multiethnic local church prepared him for leadership of a diverse network. His strategy includes creating at-large positions and using the power of appointment to "create momentum and opportunity for them to be elected." He also looks for people engaged in leadership in the marketplace to train and develop them for ministry, believing that leaders must "invest your best into your best." Further, leaders must create systems that allow people to distinguish themselves.

Allen then shared his concerns with ethnic fellowships and districts, saying that the creation of "ethnic fellowships and districts based upon language is now out of step with the culture. Labels have become inconsistent and all the lines are now blurred." He views this strategy as a disservice to the Assemblies of God. Huddleston concurred: "Integration is occurring all over the country," so the Fellowship needs a diverse lens to minister to a diverse community.

When I asked them, "How do you add multiethnicity when it is absent?" They asserted the need for a "champion," one who can serve as an advocate for the disenfranchised—racial minorities, ethnics, women, and young leaders. They also noted the need to

120

model authenticity: "We must represent who we are, organizationally and institutionally." They noted that honesty, transparency, the power of collaboration, strong interpersonal relationships, and honoring others have enabled them to promote equality and equity but acknowledged that even when doing "the right thing, with the right reason and right heart, this is still very difficult."

Duane Durst

Dr. Duane Durst, superintendent of the New York Ministry Network, began the interview by sharing about his journey moving from Ohio to pastor in New York City.[5] His church was "plain as vanilla" when he arrived, but over the next few years, he transformed it into a multiethnic family of faith: "We changed muggers into huggers!" He attributes the increased inclusion and diversity to sharing the power of love with others, which has attracted a rising tide of ethnics and leaders of color to the district. He explains, however, that "they are there by virtue of leadership, not by virtue of color."

He continued by describing the aggressive approach he has taken as district superintendent to cultivate minority and ethnic leaders. The district has included ethnic and minority staffing as part of their strategic planning, and he has intentionally chosen people of color to lead various events. This creates a powerful moment for others to observe these leaders' strengths and giftings.

He responds to the criticism of quotas by emphasizing the gifts that come by being both intentional and systematic: "I know firsthand the beauty of an international congregation. ... Intentionality can be demonstrated in recognizing individuals; systematically we can step back from the organization and ask what else needs to be done." He believes in the power of appointments, which can serve as an effective tool for cultivating diverse leaders, though he warned that if appointees are "simply used to check a box or somehow demonstrate that a complex issue is put to rest, then it's wrong."

Done right, however, "it can truly make a difference because you are part of the family, united by the blood of Christ." Still, Durst believes that building relationships remains the most powerful tool for cultivating leaders of color.

Daniel Miller

Daniel Miller serves as superintendent of the International Ministry Network (IMN), formerly known as the German District, which was formed in 1922 with the intention of reaching German immigrants with the Pentecostal message."[6] He began by sharing a story of his calling, over thirty-one years ago to pastor First Assembly of God, Benton Harbor, Michigan, now known as Blue Roof Church. After his candidate sermon, the church's board took him on a tour of the area, which reminded him of the Charles Dicken's story, *A Tale of Two Cities*. St. Joseph, a predominately white, affluent, and prosperous nearby sister city, had beautiful homes, a quaint downtown, and beachfront properties on Lake Michigan. In contrast, however, Benton Harbor, with its nearly all black residents, showed both its age and neglect, with boarded homes, slums, and an inner city in disrepair. In that moment, he knew God had called him to bridge these two communities.

When I asked him what systems he implemented to achieve a now racially diverse congregation, he noted that he just "loved people in." He acknowledges the difficulty of the journey and how he lost many along the way, but he knew racial diversity remained the right way forward for his church. This experience at the church provided a prophetic picture of what would take place in the district: "When I took over as superintendent, I thought my role was to close the German District. At this point we only had twelve churches and about twenty credential holders. Now, with God's help, we have forty churches and nearly eighty-five credential holders." Highly diverse, the IMN comprises a variety of multiethnic churches— African-American, Burmese, Hispanic, and African.

Miller described three values he espouses for the district as it pertains to cultivating racial diversity:

1. Diversity—"Diversity is close to the heart of God! We want our district to look like heaven. This value is demonstrated in our district leadership. Our secretary-treasurer is black; our presbytery is comprised of a white female, a Cuban, and a Mexican."

2. Intentionality—"Flowing from our value of diversity, we are intentional about ensuring that diversity reflects in all that we do, from our district council speakers to those on the platform leading in worship." During the IMN 2019 district council, the opening night featured a Hispanic celebration, with a Spanish worship team and Melissa Alfaro as the speaker. They followed this with black worship leader, Pastor Shawn Branham from Columbus, Ohio, and a message from Rick DuBose.

3. Relationships—Many within the network call Miller "father," reflecting his relational approach. He says, "People are hungry for relationship. They are hungry to be loved and hungry for connections." He shared how the IMN highly values personal connections. During their bi-annual IMN Connect Event, the district rents a large home to accommodate about forty attendees. This minister's retreat allows people to share space and spend a week in fellowship and prayer to spiritually invest in one another.

---

[1] See Appendix C, "Great Lakes Cohort Session Two."
[2] Rich Guerra, interview with author, February 14, 2019, Puerto Vallarta, Mexico. See Appendix H, "Interview with Rich Guerra."
[3] Sam Huddleston, interview with author, February 14, 2019, Puerto Vallarta, Mexico. See Appendix I, "Interview with Sam Huddleston."
[4] Brent Allen and Sam Huddleston, interview with author, February 14, 2019, Puerto Vallarta, Mexico. See Appendix J, "Interview with Brent Allen and Samuel Huddleston."
[5] Duane Durst, interview with author via telephone, February 6, 2019.
[6] Daniel Miller, interview with author, February 14, 2019, Puerto Vallarta, Mexico.

10 Final Thoughts

Introduction

The goal of this book was to provide resources to encourage leaders within the Assemblies of God to cultivate leadership opportunities for black leaders. The biblical-theological chapters of Section One provided the **orthodoxy** of that endeavor. They not only detailed the biblical principles of cultivation, but also examined what happens when righteous outsiders receive opportunities to lead—God works with them and through them.

Sections Two and Three delved into the **orthopraxy** of cultivating leadership opportunities for black leaders, beginning with an historical overview and brief discussion of social challenges, moving on to suggested models for building diverse and inclusive organizations, and including training materials related to the Appreciative Inquiry process and valuable perspectives from innovative leaders concerning minority leadership in the Assemblies of God.

This concluding chapter reflects on strengths of my pilot project and suggests areas for improvement as well as recommendations for the Fellowship and for future research.

Evaluation of the Project

Keys to Project Effectiveness

Doug Clay Interview

The first key to this project's success came from General Superintendent of the Assemblies of God, Doug Clay, who agreed to an in-person interview with me at the AG National Leadership and Resource Center (NLRC). Though newly-elected at the time and busy transitioning to his new role, he did not hesitate to schedule a meeting with me. The conversation that ensued proved invaluable as he provided critical insights and advice on how to implement certain components of this project. His strong affirmation for the need for diversity in leadership, referrals of innovative leaders, and his recommendation that I work with the Great Lakes Regional Superintendent Cohort provided much needed structure as I planned and implemented my field research.

Innovative Leaders Interview

The innovative leaders I interviewed also contributed significantly to the success of this project. With the exception of one interview, which I conducted via telephone, I met with each leader in person, allowing me to not only hear their hearts but also see the sincerity in their faces, underscoring the value of this project. Their passion, vision, and commitment to cultivating organizations that value diversity and inclusion proved refreshing. They provided critical perspectives on the topic of diversity in the Fellowship, and they told priceless stories on how they overcame various barriers to diversity.

The black community likes to say about those in power that some "get it" and others "don't get it." In other words, those who get it do not require a lot of convincing that a problem exists as it pertains to a lack of diverse leadership, which requires intentional solutions. Thankfully, the innovative leaders I interviewed get it. Their practices reflect a fresh pragmatism that remains unentangled by the high weeds of fear, complacency, or indecision. The candor, transparency, and vulnerability they demonstrated in their interviews provided much-needed support and inspiration for the second workshop I would later conduct.

Great Lakes Superintendents Cohort

The Great Lakes Regional Superintendent Cohort remained critical for the success of this project. This great team of leaders willingly welcomed me into two of their annual retreats. They engaged in a high level of honest reflection and sharing, which provided critical and challenging perspectives on diverse leadership. The observations they made during the process of appreciative inquiry revealed some of the concerns they have in finding the most effective ways to increase leadership diversity. In revealing some of the issues they struggle with, they confirmed the need for the very existence of this project.

National Black Fellowship (NBF) Assistance with Black Credential Holder Survey

Administering the Black Credential Holders Survey yielded highly insightful yet somewhat conflicting information. Due to confidentiality concerns, the General Secretary's office could not provide me contact information for the Fellowship's black credential holders, which severely limited my ability to contact a broad range of African American AG ministers. However, I compensated for this by contacting the Assemblies of God National Black Fellowship, which maintains their own database of contact emails. The NBF assisted me with sending out the survey to their members. Without their assistance, I would not have been able to administer the survey to as many people as I did and glean the valuable information the survey provided.

The National Black Fellowship

The National Black Fellowship provided the most valuable key to the success of this project. For over twenty years, I have remained involved with the National Black Fellowship. My personal mentor and spiritual father, the late Bishop Burton Ross, had participated in the NBF during its formative years, and he mentored me to later serve in NBF leadership. Since 2013, I have served as an executive officer, first as executive treasurer and then as vice president. Though I did not make the NBF the singular focus of this project, it provided me with a lens to observe the issues and struggles encapsulated within the project. The NBF helped me see beyond my initial focus on the local church that I pastor and recognize the broader issues affecting minority leaders across the entire Assemblies of God in the United States.

The National Black Fellowship gave me the vision to see that the issues surrounding the cultivation of African American leaders needed a voice; this helped me understand my responsibility as an individual of color to explore these issues for my project. My peer group with the NBF dropped nuggets of truth that became a catalyst of sorts, rousing me to this project: Michael Nelson asked, "Why do we fly over black babies in America to reach babies in Africa?" Walter Harvey declared, "America's inner cities just didn't happen. While the Church slept, the enemy sowed tares amongst the wheat." And Darrell Geddes asked, "What does it truly mean to be a black church today?" Without these questions and challenging assertions, this project would have taken an entirely different course.

Keys to Project Improvement

A More Practical Design

Often, when Doctor of Ministry candidates select their project, candidates have the organizational influence to oversee the implementation of change. However, in the case of this project, I had no such influence, which turned this project into one of raising awareness about the need to cultivate diversity rather than a project that implemented visible change in leadership. Thus, one way to have improved this project would have been to seek a single district and invest effort and resources in working with the leadership team to increase diversity.

This project remains in need of strong partners working in a test lab of sorts, one in which a leader has the capacity and influence to practically deploy the truths discovered by this project. The subject of this project remains profoundly significant. At times, my research and field implementation drastically affected my emotions and my thinking. Sometimes I responded in anger, other times in frustration, and often in tears. This project needs the hands of someone with the right heart and capacity to open the door and implement it in practical ways.

Addressing Other Minorities

Further, as I evaluate the entire project, I realize I should have broadened the focus beyond African American leaders. A more effective approach would have examined how to cultivate leadership opportunities for all minorities. Changing the focus to include other minorities would have given this project more agility and appeal to a wider spectrum of leaders, not just black leaders.

Increased Discussion of Biblical Justice

This project would have also benefitted from increased discussion on the theme of biblical justice. While the general literature review briefly mentioned the concept of broken windows, I did not explore the connection between biblical social justice and cultivating opportunities for diverse leadership, an observation of a Gen X classmate and friend who heard tales of racial injustices from the elders of my family. As Millennials have risen into leadership, civil rights issues seem like they belong to bygone days; however, younger people have deep passion for justice issues. Though they may not see the relevancy of conversations related to civil rights, they do see and understand issues discussed through the lens of justice. The concept of justice links the history of the Civil Rights Movement to the contemporary conscience of younger leaders.

More Diverse Survey Respondents

Though I remain indebted to the National Black Fellowship for assisting me in sending out the Black Credential Holders Survey to their constituents, NBF constituents already remain highly engaged in various levels of leadership. As such, they may not accurately reflect the experiences of other black leaders, who may experience difficulty serving in leadership roles. Lingering questions remain as to whether the results of the survey genuinely reflect the larger body of black leaders or if these responses represent a pool of ideal and involved leaders. If the Assemblies of God as a fellowship would allow credential holders to opt-in for contact on matters related to research and dissertation projects, such access would help both the researcher and the Fellowship as well. A wider pool of participants would have provided a more objective voice.

Appreciative Inquiry Workshops

The participants of the appreciative inquiry workshops consisted of district superintendents, who came to the workshops with certain perceptions of black leaders' engagement in the Fellowship. As a result, the broad nature of my approach made the workshops more participative rather than collaborative. On reflection, I would have still held the workshops with the cohort of superintendents, but I would have accompanied this with the support and partnership of one district as well. By partnering with one district and gaining their leadership support, the project would have likely benefited from producing actionable change.

Conclusion

My doctoral journey and the adaptation of that material into this book has been a transformational journey resulting in a practical tool for action that has a strong biblical basis for inclusive leadership and that takes into consideration the contemporary challenges to achieving that goal.

Jesus declares, "My house shall be called a house of prayer for all the nations" (Mark 11:17, ESV). He did not leave anyone out in that statement. Building inclusive, multi-ethnic organizations is not simply a trendy issue for postmodern leaders seeking relevancy. Inclusive leadership reflects the heart of God. As the Church seeks to please Him, it must not miss the crucial moment to capture His heart and cultivate leadership opportunities for minorities at all levels of the organization.

About the Author

Rev. Dr. Darnell K. Williams, Sr

Beginnings. A native of Cleveland, Ohio, Darnell grew up in a single parent home. With an incredible support system, lots of determination, and the grace of God, he was able to push beyond the pains of his childhood and pursue God's plan for his life. Dr. Darnell accepted Christ at sixteen years old and began ministry at nineteen.

Ministry. He was ordained to the gospel ministry in 1992. Currently, he serves as senior pastor of New Life Church International, a multiethnic ministry in Lima, Ohio (since 2006). He holds ordination credentials with the Assemblies of God.

Education. He holds an earned Doctor of Ministry with the Assemblies of God Theological Seminary, Springfield, MO.

Professionally. His business background spans the areas of Banking, Credit Card, Mortgage, and Insurance.

Leadership. Dr. Darnell serves as Secretary-Treasurer of the International Ministry Network (German District) of the Assemblies of God; General Presbyter of the Assemblies of God (by virtue of office); and Vice President of the National Black Fellowship of the Assemblies of God. He was elected to serves as an Executive Presbyter at the 58th General Council of the Assemblies of God.

Serving in the capacity of Bishop, Williams provides oversight to the New Life Network, a relational gathering of churches and para-church ministries.

Community. Dr. Darnell serves as a member of the Rhodes State College University Foundation Board (Since 2015). He also serves as a Trustee for Evangel University (Since 2016). He serves as the President of Judah Enterprises, non-profit ministry that provides outreach to families facing food insecurities and ministering compassion to those in need. Likewise, he has served as Chaplain for Lima Memorial health systems and the Lima Police Department.

Family. He has been happily married (since 1993) to K. Charlene Williams of Guyana, South America, who serves with him in ministry. They are the proud parents of a son in college, Adrian.

CPSIA information can be obtained
at www.ICGtesting.com
Printed in the USA
JSHW041545180121
11003JS00004B/19